INSIGHT POCKET GUIDES

CRETE

APA PUBLICATIONS

ΜΝΗΜΕΙΑ ΤΗΣ ΕΛΛΑΔΑΣ
MONUMENTS OF GREECE

MNE 1767238

Παρακαλείστε να κρατήσετε το απόκομμα του εισιτηρίου σας
μέχρι την έξοδό σας από το χώρο.
You are requested to preserve your ticket until you leave the Museum/Site.

ΕΙΣΙΤΗΡΙΟ
ΕΙΣΟΔΟΥ

ΔΡΧ. 500
DRS.

ENTRANCE
TICKET

GRAPHIC ARTS CHAR. I. PAPADOPOULOS S.A.

BULGARIA
Edirne
Lüleburgaz
Corlu
ISTANBU
Drama
Serres
Xanthi
Komotini
Kilkis
Kavala
Keşan
Tekirdağ
Alexandroupoli
Marmara Denizi
Thessaloniki
Kalamaria
Stratoni
THASOS
HALKIDIKI
Gerakini
SAMOTHRAKI
Gelibolu
Bandirma
Canakkale
AG. OROS
Gönen
M. Kemalpaşa
SITHONIA
KASSANDRA
LIMNOS
Balikesir
AG. EFSTRA-
-TIOS
NORTHERN SPORADES
Edremit
Volos
GIOURA
PIPERI
SKIATHOS
LESVOS
Mithimna
ALONNISOS
Soma
TURKEY
SKANDZOURA
Bergama
(Pergamon)
SKOPELOS
Mytilini
Loutra Edipsou
Akhisar
SKIROPOULA
A
SKYROS
Manisa
EUBOEA
Paralia Kimis
e
Livadia
Thiva
(Theben)
Halkida
PSARA
Karsiyaka
Thiva
(Thebes)
Kalamos
Chios
Izmir
Alasehir
GREECE
g
Urla
Ödemis
HIOS
Megara
Karistos
e
CHIOS
Küçük Menderes
Athens
Korinthos
Piraeus
Vouliagmeni
ANDROS
a
SAMOS
Selçuk
Aydin
Nazilli
AEGINA
Samos
Büyük Menderes
KEA
GIAROS
IKARIA
Söke
Saronikos Kolpos
Sounio
TINOS
n
FOURNI
Altburgazi
Epidavros
ARKI
Portoheli
MYKONOS
LIPSI
Milàs
IDRA
(HYDRA)
SYROS
PATMOS
Argolikos Kolpos
KITHNOS
SPETSES
PAROS
NAXOS
LEROS
Güllük
Muğla
SERIFOS
LEVITHA
Kiparissi
SIPHNOS
KEROS
KALIMNOS
KIMOLOS
KOS
Marmaris
AMORGOS
CYCLADES
IOS
GIALI
Reşadiye
Monemvasia
MILOS
ASTIPALEA
DODECANESE
FOLE-
GANDROS
SIKINOS
NISIROS
SANTORINI
(THERA)
SYMI
Rodos
THERASIA
ANAFI
TILOS
ALIMIA
Kithira
KITHIRA
HALKI
RHODES
Lindos
Sea of Crete
SARIA
ANDIKITHIRA
Plátanos
Chaniá
KARPATHOS
Irákleion
KASOS
Réthymnon
Knossós
Aghios Nikólaos
Paleóhora
CRETE
Sitia
Ag. Galíni
Míres
Ierápetra
Greece
(The Aegean)
100 km

Welcome!

An island of infinite variety, Crete has something for everyone – attractive resorts where new development doesn't detract from ochre-coloured old quarters; a fascinating blend of Greek and Ottoman influences, as seen in minarets that now serve as belfries; ancient ruins, including the famous site of Knossós; idyllic beaches; and rural villages where traditional lifestyles prevail. It is the largest and most legendary of the Greek Islands, the supposed birthplace of Zeus and the centre of the Minoan civilisation of 3000BC.

In the following pages *Insight Guides'* correspondent on Crete helps you make the most of your stay there. In a series of carefully crafted itineraries based on the four main regions of Chaniá, Réthymnon, Irákleion and Lassíthi, she guides visitors to all the main sights and prises out many hidden gems, from wild ravines and mountain *tavernes* to a cave monastery perched high above the sea.

Brigitte von Seckendorff-Kourgierákis has lived on Crete since 1961. She has seen many changes in that time but sees Crete's tourist expansion as yet another step in its evolution. In preparing this book she crisscrossed the island many times, travelling hundreds of kilometres along gravel roads and building on her own knowledge of Crete by tapping the knowledge of her friends. On her journeys she shared food and wine with many well-wishing Cretans and listened to their tales and myths, recognising again and again the sheer magic that first drew her here.

CONTENTS

History & Culture

Crete's Highlights

A selection of 24 full-day and half-day itineraries divided according to Crete's main regions.

CHANIA

Pages 2/3: the fortress of Irákleion

RÉTHYMNON

IRAKLEION

Pages 8/9: the waterfront at Chaniá

HISTORY &

From Minóa to King Mínos

Crete (*Ee Kreétee* in Greek) was, in antiquity, densely forested with cypress, cedar, oak, juniper and plain trees, as well as various varieties of pines and palms. In his poetry, Homer refers to 'Knossós of the many trees' as well as to the heavily wooded Mount Ida range. Crete was a green paradise which did not actually become an island until around a million years ago, when segments of the mountain range connecting the Peleponnese (southern Greece) with what today is Turkey sank below sea level. Where did the first human settlers of the region come from? The scientific community has not yet reached a consensus on this point, but they probably originated in Asia Minor, Africa or, perhaps, predynastic Egypt. Whatever the origins of the first Cretans, the island was populated during the Neolithic Age as early as the 7th century BC.

Schliemann's discovery of Troy, which established the historical validity of Homer's epic poetry, followed by the discovery of Knossós by the Cretan scholar Kalokerinós, triggered off a veritable frenzy of excavation. Digging at Knossós between 1900 and 1903, the

The Palace of Knossós

Culture

English archaeologist Arthur Evans made a crucial discovery. Instead of the expected Mycenaean remains, Evans unearthed a great building complex, a palace, which he recognised to be the centre of an even older civilisation. He proceeded to name this 'new' culture 'Minoan', after that powerful and wily monarch of Greek mythology, King Mínos, though no image of him ever turned up at Knossós, nor any other evidence that a 'King Mínos' had played a central role in the culture which was to bear his name.

'The King of Priests'

What Evans did find were renderings, in various media, of decidedly female figures. After initially trivialising them, he eventually concluded 'that we are looking at a great monotheistic cult in which the female form of deity occupied the highest position…' The Minoan goddess, a sister of the moon- and mother-goddesses of Asia Minor, later metamorphosed into the Greek goddess Rhea. Her symbol was the double axe, or 'labrys'; trees were consecrated to her; and she was also worshipped in the form of a snake in private homes.

In around 3000BC, paralleling the civilisations of Egypt and Mesopotamia, a great culture evolved on Crete which is thought to have been the first such flowering in Europe. The older 'palaces', erected in around the year 2000, were destroyed some 300 years later. Subsequently, new, similar complexes were built atop the ruins on the same sites. The 'palaces' were major economic, political and religious centres, and Homer placed their number at 100. Multi-storeyed, they included workshops, large storerooms, places of worship, areas reserved for social functions, courtyards, theatres, plumbing and sewage facilities as well as projecting and receding façades. Later Greek conquerers of Crete were so bewildered by this architecture that they coined the word 'labyrinth' – from 'House of Labrys'. The Minoan system of writing – in hieroglyphs and syllabary form – has been only partially deciphered, but a culture capable of developing writing and such sophisticated art and architectural forms as those of the Minoans may be considered to have attained a high level of civilisation and prosperity.

Fresco from Knossós

As early as the 12th century BC, the Dorians, a rough breed of uneducated semi-barbarians, were on the advance throughout Greece, bringing war to the once peaceful island and enslaving its inhabitants. The Minoans, men and women alike, retreated into the mountains, founding new cities there. From this point on, Crete belonged firmly in the Greek world. The Greek goddesses and gods supplanted the island deities – above all, the divine Olympian patriarch, Zeus, whose birthplace Crete was thought to be. Zeus became immortal along the same lines as the partner of the Great Goddess: he died or was sacrificed in the autumn and then rose again in the spring. As this heretical belief in Zeus's 'resurrection' was incomprehensible to the mainland Greeks they defamed the Cretans, coining the maxim 'All Cretans are liars'.

Foreign Intervention

During the 1st century, the Roman commander Metallus acquired the epithet 'Creticus' by breaking the Cretans' stalwart three-year resistance, incorporating them into the Roman Empire. The island then became the granary of the empire and an important military base, as well as ripe ground for the spread of Christianity. During the 7th and 8th centuries, Rome was subjected to increasingly effective attacks by the Slavs, Persians and Arabs.

Land of ruins

Finally, in 1204, in a very understated transaction, Crete was sold to the Republic of Venice for 10,000 silver marks. The indigenous people put up a bitter resistance for 200 years but did not succeed in throwing off foreign rule.

After the conquest of Constantinople by the Turks in 1453, many intellectuals and artists fled to Crete, which led to a final florescence of Byzantine art and culture on the island, influenced by the Italian Renaissance. The painters Domenikos Theotokópoulos ('El Greco') and Michaïl Damaskinós belong to this period, as do the poet Vitzéntzios Kornáros, author of the epic drama *Erotókritós*, and the playwright Yiórgios Chortátzis.

Candia, as the Venetians called the modern capital of Irákleion, the most formidable fortress in the Mediterranean, was forced to surrender to the Turks in 1669. Islamisation made rapid progress. The so-called *Turkokrítes* were Cretans, as far as their clothing, language and customs were concerned, but they professed the Muslim faith. The island was divided up among pashas and large landowners, trade and agriculture fell off and the Renaissance ended.

Despite these demoralising developments for Crete the Turkish forces were faced with constant resistance. This period of struggle, a time of mass executions and rebellion, is kept alive in many stories still told on the island; and in songs singing the praises of those 'brave young men', the *palikária*, and their feminine counterparts, the *levéntisses*.

The year 1821 marked the beginning of the struggle on the Greek mainland for liberation from the Ottoman yoke – up in 'old Greece', as elderly Cretans still often call it. While Greece became a free state, at least on paper, the Turks continued to suppress savagely all rebellion on Crete. In 1866, 1,000 people, barricaded in the Arkádi Monastery, ignited an ammunition dump and blew themselves up rather than fall into the hands of the Turks besieging them. When an additional massacre of Christians in Irákleion took place, the English consul was among those killed and the European powers responded with outrage, sending in ships and declaring Crete autonomous. As a result, the Turkish military was forced to leave, but the island remained under Turkish sovereignty.

The Turkish fortress of Aptera

In 1899, the first Cretan government was sworn in: Elefthérios Venizélos, Chaniá's favourite son and later prime minister of Greece, was named Minister of Justice. For a brief period, Chaniá became a small European capital – acquiring the cosmopolitan flair which it has retained until today.

Meanwhile, the island was 'protected' by international armed forces: the Nomós, or Prefecture, of Chaniá by the Italians; Nomós Réthymnon by the Russians; Nomós Irákleion by the English, and Nomós Lassíthi by the French. This authoritarian system paved the way for another revolution in 1905, but Crete did not become part of the Greek state until 1913, since which time it has remained a stronghold of progressively-orientated parties, from the Liberals and the Cretan Party to today's PASOK, the Greek socialists.

In 1913, King Constantine and Prime Minister Venizélos came to Chaniá to proclaim Crete's official union with Greece. The remaining Turkish population, some 33,000 strong, had to leave the island immediately.

The Air Invasion

Four days after Greece surrendered to the German military, 20 May 1941, marked the beginning of one of the most bitter chapters in Cretan history. This was when Hitler launched operation 'Merkur', which involved dropping thousands of German soldiers by parachute onto Crete in order to capture it as a supply base for the Africa Corps. Before the soldiers were able to free themselves from their parachutes, however, they made easy targets for British and Cretan soldiers, the latter armed primarily with knives and clubs. The retaliation of the German Wehrmacht was swift: villages were razed, cities bombed and male inhabitants executed. Memorial plaques all over Crete testify to these tragic events.

On 11 October 1944, Irákleion was handed over to the Cretan partisans. Western Crete, however, remained occupied by German forces until 8 May 1945.

Cretan villagers began their migration to the cities during the

German military cemetery at Máleme

Religious fresco

1950s, moving to Athens or abroad in search of employment. Today, it is difficult to find a family without relatives in America, Australia or Germany.

In 1951, the United States built military bases near Chaniá and Irákleion. A new occupation had begun – controversial and much criticised since. Another 'invasion', this time in the form of the Colonels' military dictatorship, also affected Crete. During the junta, from 1967 to 1974, many islanders were persecuted, imprisoned and tortured along with liberals and democrats throughout the rest of Greece.

Resistance, in one guise or another, has long been the central theme in Crete's history, since the decline of the peaceful Minoan society till today. The much-sung, often banned Cretan 'anthem' expresses the islanders' longing for freedom and peace in such lines as: 'When will the sky be free of clouds? When will February come; spring…?' But considering Crete's pivotal geographical position between Africa, Asia and Europe, poised above the turbulent Middle East, a future free of foreign intervention seems unlikely.

The Extended Cretan Family

In spite of increasing urbanisation and the staggering boom in tourism, the four regions of Crete, blocked off by three imposing massifs, have maintained their own customs and dialects. The period of migration is over, and some of the emigrants have even begun to return. Since 1971, the population has steadily increased to its present level of 520,000. Today, tourism, agriculture, trade and industry provide enough jobs to keep the Cretans at home.

The island has also become an attractive destination for Athenians keen on escaping the polluted capital with its smog, traffic and overcrowding. Intellectual life on Crete is characterised by the multitude of cultural associations, as well as by the university, founded in 1977. Since the school maintains separate campuses in Chaniá, Réthymnon and Irákleion, wags sometimes call it 'the longest university in the world'.

With its tight network of social relationships, Cretan society retains the feeling of one big extended family. The Greek tradition of *koumbariá*, a sort of elective kinship system involving 'best men' and godfathers, creates inter-relationships as binding as those based on blood. For the Cretan politician intent on securing a following and consolidating power, it is essential to stand in as godfather to as many island children as possible. It is this that makes him a *sínteknos*, a co-parent. By sharing the responsibility for a child, he acquires a new family (of voters). In this scheme of things, weddings and baptisms are highly significant social events. Often attended by hundreds of guests, there is always plenty of eating, drinking and dancing at these celebrations.

The *paniyíria*, or saints' day festivities, are also important occasions. On the eve of the celebrations, people throng to the church or monastery sacred to the saint to light their candles in anticipation of the feast day to follow. The Greek Orthodox Church has always played an important role on Crete and continues to do so. During the centuries of foreign rule, it was the Church which preserved the Greek language and culture, and the priests played a leading role in the Cretan resistance.

On Crete, time, as we know it in the West, does not exist. 'Right away', 'soon', and 'in five minutes' are assurances that can rarely be taken at face value. They may just as well mean 'in half an hour'. Information concerning distances should also be treated with a healthy dollop of suspicion, along with street directions. The Cretan clock marches to a very different drummer. Long mornings are followed by siesta time which lasts from around 2 until at least 5pm, when the Cretans rise and the 'afternoon' begins. Shops reopen, employees return to their offices, lawyers and physicians resume their practices, and people pay visits.

At about 8pm it is time for the evening stroll, or *vólta*. A sort of 'see and be seen parade', the *vólta* has long served as the village marriage market, with prospective brides and suitors displaying their wealth and advertising their availability in shady squares or over cups of Greek coffee at seaside cafés. The rest of the evening, from 9pm on, is spent at the cinema, the theatre, at a concert or dining with one's special circle of friends, one's *paréa*, or relatives. Cretans may even schedule dinner for much later. It is a relaxed

Sitía's city centre

social event that is never rushed, and *'Na seh kerásso'* ('Let me serve, or treat, you') is the first sentence you should learn in Greek. It is the key to polite social behaviour in the land of hospitality. When Cretans sit down to dine, no one would think of refilling only his own wineglass. First, you serve your companions; then yourself. Hospitality is extended just as naturally as it is expected in return.

The Tourist Trade

Crete has the largest amount of tourist trade of all the Mediterranean islands, with a 14 percent growth rate. From April to October well over a million holiday-makers visit the island. Germans predominate, followed by Scandinavians and English.

The travel craze has two sides. On the one hand, it produces a certain affluence and is therefore welcomed by the islanders. On the other hand, the locals view the overwhelming influx of summer visitors as a kind of hostile occupation force. Often the much-praised Cretan hospitality is at risk of degenerating into a simple business arrangement, with the visitors contributing their share to this sad development. It is difficult for tourists to understand the rules of hospitality in an alien culture, and well-meaning guests may fail to reciprocate kindness tendered by Cretans. What becomes more and more difficult as a result of this eroded relationship between guests and hosts is achieving any real access to the people and their island, especially in the main resorts.

Tourist ghettos have evolved, entire towns avoided by the local population and abandoned in winter. This precludes the very dialogue and exchange which the enlightened traveller seeks wherever he goes; the meeting of minds that is the first, essential step in understanding the history and culture of Crete. An afternoon in a so-called 'real' Cretan village, built specifically for tourists, or an organised 'Cretan Evening' are no substitutes for the sort of encounter that is today difficult to experience if one stays in a resort. However, take off for the hills and the chances are your journey will be filled with unexpected invitations (to sample home-made wine, to admire a special view or to join in a local feast) and showered with small presents (a bag of walnuts, a dish of apricots, a cup of sweet black coffee with some freshly baked biscuits).

As throughout all of Greece, music and song play an integral role in Cretan life. The oldest Cretan songs are the *risítika.* Written

Bathing fun at Chersónissos

in the foothills of the Lefka Ori, the White Mountains, as early as the 10th century, they have since spread throughout the island. They are meant to be sung at the *távla*, the richly decked table, but also on the *stráta*, the street – on the occasion of the 'collecting' of the bride, for example. The songs recount heroic deeds, dreams of freedom, the beauty of the bride, and other stock themes of Cretan life. Popular songs at parties are *matináthes*, whose lyrics consist of rhythmic couplets, often composed on the spot, with everyone joining in for the chorus.

The principal musical instruments in use on Crete today are of Byzantine or Arabian origin: the *lyra*, a three-stringed, plucked instrument, and the accompanying lute. Larger ensembles, however, also use the violin, mandolin, guitar, bagpipes, wind instruments and small drums, whereas the straight flute, perhaps the oldest of Cretan musical instruments, has all but disappeared.

The place to go if you want to listen to indigenous music, dance and have a good meal while you are at it is a *kritikó kéntro*, one of those large restaurant-clubs catering for weddings and other celebrations, located outside the towns. The Cretan dances are elegant and fast: the *sirtós*, *pentosáli* and *malevisiótikos* are all round dances; only the *soústa*, which dates from the Venetian occupation, is danced by couples.

Musical ensemble

Crete is, in fact, one large mountain range, and its people were once semi-nomadic, mounting mules and riding up to the highland villages in summer. The many weekend outings with one's *paréa* usually end on Sunday evening in the *kafeníon* of a mountain village or at the home of a *koumbáros* or *sínteknos* who has prepared *kokinistó*, a kid goat steamed in a wine and tomato sauce; boiled *stamnangáthia*, a type of wild dandelion and the most expensive wild vegetable on Crete; and *paximáthia*, double-baked barley rusks soaked in water, then covered in oil and tomatoes and generously sprinkled with *rígani*, wild oregano. The repast may also include the hard cheese, *graviéra*, and the finest Greek soft cheese, *athótiros*. To drink with the meal, you have a choice of wine from the barrel, the locally brewed beer or the local brand of anise-flavoured schnapps, *tsigouthía*, practically the Cretan 'national' drink.

In the streets of Cretan towns and villages, one still occasionally sees an elderly man in boots and baggy breeches, a crocheted, fringed scarf tied artlessly around his head – the antique garb of Moslem and Christian Cretans both. The men's beautiful old regional costumes, with their finely embroidered waistcoats, and the elaborate gowns of the women are today worn only at staged events or consigned to folklore museums. Young Cretans, like their Western counterparts, prefer the international uniform of jeans, athletic shoes, T-shirts and jackets embossed with famous labels.

However, at the same time, the Orthodox priest, the *papás*, in his long black soutane and conical hat is by no means unusual, especially now that he is allowed to wear his hair and beard short. He may be married – only the higher-level clergy remain celibate – have children and as a rule he knows quite well what life in the real world is like.

There are plenty of reasons for wanting to visit Crete, but once you have, a return trip is inevitable for you will be smitten. In the words of Nobel prize winner, Odysséus Elytis, who was born in Irákleion in 1911: 'Take me, take me to Crete, and do not ask, do not ask me why.'

Ierápetra, south coast city

Historical Highlights

6500–3000BC Neolithic Age. First settlers arrive from Asia Minor or North Africa.

3000–2050 Prepalatial Period. Processing of copper and use of the potter's wheel.

2050–1625 Early Palatial Period. Discovery of bronze, written language developed. Destruction of the old palaces.

1625–1375 The Late Palatial Period, and Late Minoan era. Minoan culture dominates the seas. Palaces are destroyed in 1375.

1375–1000 Post-Palatial Period. Crete participates in the Trojan War. Beginning of the Iron Age, marked by the arrival of the Dorians and the retreat of the Eteocretans into the mountains.

1000–67 Dark Ages. Founding of Dorian towns and constant internecine feuding. In 145, Pressós, largest Eteocretan town and largest pirates' lair in the Eastern Mediterranean, falls.

67BC–AD337 Crete becomes a Roman province under Metallus 'Creticus'. Górtis becomes capital city and Christianity spreads. Titos named first bishop of Crete.

337–826 Crete's first Byzantine period, following the division of Rome. Crete falls to Byzantium and pirate raids become rife.

827–961 Arabs occupy Crete, destroying Górtis and founding Rabdh el Khandak (Irákleion), where a slave market flourishes.

961–1204 Second Byzantine Period. Crete reconquered by Byzantine General Phokás, era of military administration, rechristianisation and establishment of the feudal system. Sea trade is in the hands of the Genoese, the capital is called Chándax (Irákleion).

1204–1669 Venice purchases Crete, expelling the Genoese, and renaming Chándax Candia. Venetian colonists flood in, but their rule is marked by uprisings, corsair raids and expanded fortifications. All but Candia eventually conquered by the Ottoman Turks.

1669–1898 Turkish dominance. Candia falls to the Turks in 1770 after a 20-year siege. An uprising led by Daskaloyánnis is suppressed.

1821–28 Crete participates in the Greek struggle for independence. In 1850, Chaniá becomes capital; in 1866, the tragedy at Arkádi Monastery occurs, leading to further popular uprisings.

1889–1913 Some autonomy is gained when, still under the Sultan, the island is protected by the major European powers. Moslem Cretans leave. Crete redoubles its efforts to join Greece.

1913–41 Crete unites with Greece following the Balkan Wars, entering World War I on the side of the Entente. Turks leave in 1923.

1941–5 The German Occupation, heavy losses, destruction of many villages and mass executions.

1944–9 Greek Civil War is fought less fiercely than on the mainland.

1967–74 Military dictatorship.

1972 Irákleion becomes the capital of Crete.

1981 Greece joins the EC; elects a socialist government helped by Crete's massive left-wing support.

1996 Post-dictatorship era ends with the death of the charismatic socialist leader Andreas Papandreou, the last of the old generation of post-war politicians. The phlegmatic Kostas Simitis takes over the reins of the PASOK party and leads it to election victory.

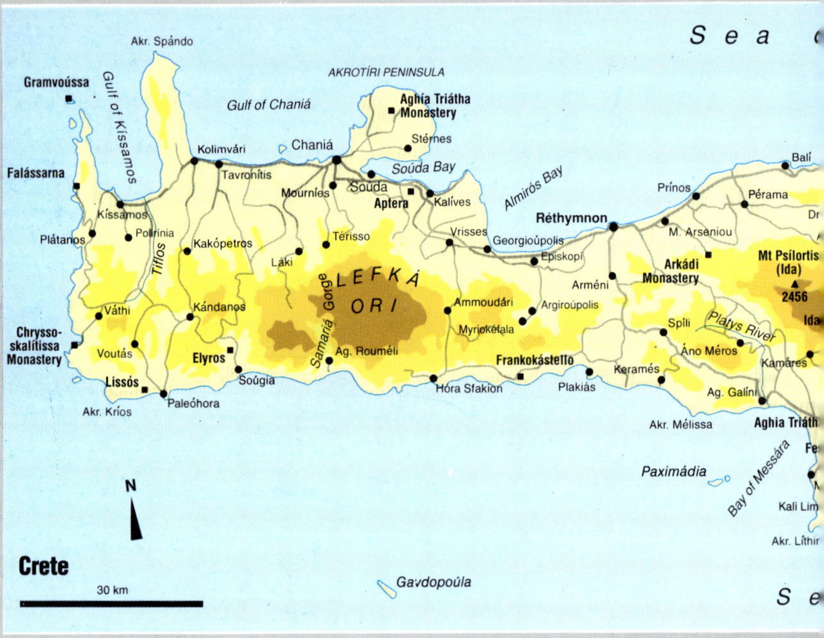

Sea
Akr. Spándo
AKROTÍRI PENINSULA
Gramvoússa
Gulf of Kíssamos
Gulf of Chaniá
Aghía Triátha Monastery
Stérnes
Chaniá
Kolimvári
Falássarna
Tavronítis
Soúda Bay
Soúda
Almirós Bay
Balí
Mournies
Aptera
Kalíves
Prínos
Pérama
Kíssamos
Réthymnon
Plátanos
Polirinia
Térisso
Vrisses
Georgioúpolis
M. Arseníou
Kakópetros
Episkopí
Mt Psílortis (Ida)
Tiflos
Laki
Arkádi Monastery
LEFKÁ ORI
Arméni
2456
Samariá Gorge
Váthi
Kándanos
Ammoudári
Argiroúpolis
Ida
Chrysso-skalítissa Monastery
Spíli
Platys River
Voutás
Myriokéfala
Áno Méros
Elyros
Ag. Rouméli
Frankokástello
Kamáres
Lissós
Soúgia
Keramés
Hora Sfakion
Plakiás
Ag. Galíni
Akr. Kríos
Paleóhora
Akr. Mélissa
Aghia Triáth
Paximádia
Bay of Messára
N
Kali Lim
Akr. Líthir
Crete
Gavdopoúla
30 km
Se

r e t e
Dia
Gulf of Irákleion
IRÁKLEION
Liménas Chersónissos
Kólpos Malion
Akr. Ag. Ioánnis
Eloúnda
SPINALONGA / KALYDÓN
Dragonáda
Akr. Síderos
Elasa
Sitía Bay
Vai
Itanós
Palékastro
Sitía
Amnissós
Knossós
Mália
Neápolis
Epáno Arhánes
Kerás
Aghios Nikólaos
Bay of Maliá
Psíra
Skopí
Meronía
Káto Zákros
Zákros
Lató
Kritsá
Stáka
Thrápsano
Díkti Cave
Psychró
Kaló Horió
Chrisopigí
Zíros
Gióftiros
DÍKTI MOUNTAINS
Gourniá
Arkalochóri
Máles
Makrigialós
Martha
Ag. Varvára
Koufonísi
Anapodáris
Protória
Ag. Árvis
Mirtos
Ierápetra
Keratókambos
Pírgos
Chrisí
f Libya

Day Itineraries

Crete is divided into four administrative regions, or *nómi*. Visitors arrive at one of the district capitals – Chaniá, Réthymnon, Irákleion or Aghios Nikólaos, the points of departure for the excursions in this guide. But please do not take any of our well-made plans too literally: an itinerary which can easily be accomplished in half a day, you yourself may wish to extend. An occasional detour off the beaten path will almost always be worth your while, even if it takes you down a bad gravel road or two.

Chaniá

Not Just Quinces and Cheese

The Arab geographer and historian Al-Sarik Al-Edrisi, who travelled throughout the island during the 12th century, reported the following: 'The island of Crete, large, densely populated and fertile, has many

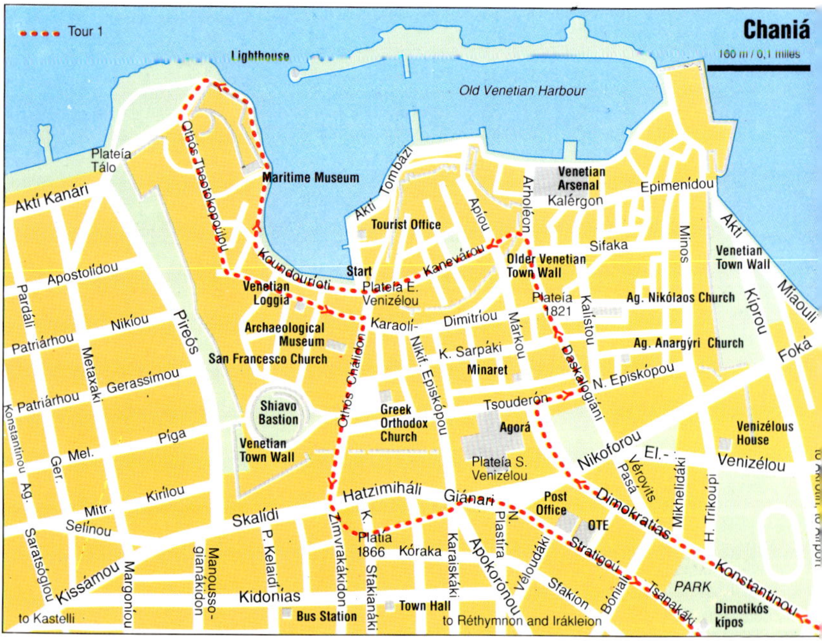

The harbour at the foot of Kastélli

flourishing cities.' One of these urban centres, surrounded by fruit orchards and hills full of wild goats, he called Rabdh-el Djobh, the 'City of Cheese'.

Chaniá's cheese still merits a mention. But 'Kydonía', the oldest name for the town, derives from the word for quince, a fruit probably introduced from Asia as early as Minoan times. In Ancient Greek myths, the entire region was said to be inhabited by the ancestors of the Kydones, ruled by King Kydon, a son of Mìnos renowned for his hospitality. Chaniá is thus one of the oldest settled areas in Europe, a fact confirmed by the discovery of an extensive settlement on the city's hill, Kydonía, in 1970. As a Roman province, Chaniá was a flourishing community, minting its own money and maintaining a theatre. Later, the Byzantines made the city the seat of a diocese. The name Chaniá may derive from *al hanim*, the Arabic word for inn. The Venetians then Italianised it, coining the name 'La Canea'.

In 1645, it was the first Cretan city to fall to the Turks, serving as an Ottoman foothold for the conquest of the rest of the island. During the next few centuries, Chaniá assumed the economic leadership of the entire island and, in 1850, became the seat of the Seraskeri Pasha, the highest pasha. Chaniá experienced its true heyday, however, as the seat of government and capital of autonomous Crete between 1898 to 1913. The quarter of Chalépa, with its fine neoclassical architecture, dates from this period.

Chaniá, Crete's capital until 1972, is growing quickly and, with its population of 63,000, is second only to Irákleion in size. It is full of vitality, with clean air and substantial recreational facilities. From here, you have easy access to the surrounding villages, to the Lefka Ori, the White Mountains, to secluded coves along the south coast, as well as to the broad sandy beaches of the West.

For characterful pensions, hotels and restaurants, in Chaniá, try the area bordering the old harbour.

1. A First Encounter

A morning exploring the old harbour and Venetian quarter; Fort Firkás; the monastery church of San Francesco and the Archaeological Museum; the joys of shopping in the covered bazaar. See the map on page 24.

The old Venetian quarter of Chaniá is classified as a protected, historic precinct and the Greek authorities have made a successful job of renovating it. At the height of summer, the quarter becomes the focal point of tourist activity in Chaniá.

You begin to get a feel for the district by setting out from **Plateía E Venizélou**, also called Sintriváni, and proceeding west along the harbour promenade (sea on your right), to the Venetian-Turkish battlements of **Fort Firkás**. This is not only the location of the **Naval Museum** (10am–4pm), which contains an exhibition of the Battle of Crete, 1941: in summer, theatre groups stage guest performances and Cretan dance evenings here. It was here that the Greek flag was raised in 1913 after the declaration of unification of Crete with Greece by Eleuthérios Venizélos and King Constantine of Greece.

From the ramparts of the fort, you have a panoramic view of the harbour, the Venetian arsenals and the former Mosque of the Janissaries, all the way to the White Mountains, 2,500m (8,202ft) high. Next to the lighthouse you can see the ruins of a fort which was the former execution site of the Venetians and Turks. There is a striking mountain slope some distance from here to the east, which Níkos Kazantzákis's hero, Alexis Zorbas – in his incarnation as Anthony Quinn – brought to the attention of the world. On a hill facing you lies **Kastélli**, the oldest district of Chaniá, with the palatial **Venetian Archives**, today part of the Technical University. West is **Aghios Theóthoros**, an island nature reserve protecting the rare Cretan wild goat, or *krí-krí*.

From the fort, walk along the shoreline road to the northern bastion of the Venetian town wall where the state-owned **Xenia Hotel** reclines and walk up **Othós Theotokopoúlou**, which is lined with pretty Turkish and Venetian houses, little craft shops and attractive restaurants.

At the end of Theotokopoúlou, turn to the left down Odós Zambeliou to rejoin the Plateía E Venizélou and then turn right up

Independence Day parade, 28 October

Fort Firkás

Othós Chálidon, the street which has the most souvenir shops. The **Archaeological Museum** (Tuesday to Sunday 8am–7pm, Monday 12.30–7pm in summer, 8am–3pm and 12.30–3pm respectively in winter) – in the former Venetian monastery church of **San Francesco** – houses interesting finds which span Crete's long and eventful history.

At the end of Othós Chálidon is **Plateía 1866**, also called Néa Katastímata, a square lined with trees, where you can find a taxi or a bus to the old seaside resort of Kalamáki.

Leaving the square, take Odós Kriari, which leads to **Plateía S Venizélou**, where you will find **Ee Agorá**, a compact shopper's paradise. Vegetables, fruit, fish, meat, spices, cheese, wine, mountain teas, snack bars and a *kafeneíon* – you can find anything and everything here. There are 78 shops and stands in all. The cross-shaped market building, begun in 1911 and unique in Greece, was patterned after the covered market in Marseille, one of Chaniá's major trading partners during the Turkish period. If you are ready for an early lunch, try the little restaurant at the far end of the market – it offers a good range of inexpensive traditional Cretan dishes. It has a few tables and chairs on the terrace outside.

Opposite the market **Othós Tzanakáki** begins, its upper part lined with trees and beautiful neoclassical architecture. This is one of the city's main streets, and the post office, telephone exchange (OTE), travel agencies, Olympic Airways and many small boutiques, are located here. The **Dimotikós Kípos** (Municipal Gardens), a park featuring a gorgeous, old-style *kafeneíon*, is an inviting place in which to

Back-street charm

relax over a drink; its open-air cinema is a popular destination for Chaniá's movie lovers in summer.

Out of the park, take the first left and left again onto **Othós Dimokratías** which leads back to the market. Northeast of the Agorá (walk along its near side then turn right down Odós Tsouderon and left down Odós Daskalogiani) is **Plateía 1821**, the centre of the former Turkish Quarter, surrounded by Turkish coffee houses and overlooked by the minaret of what used to be the Sultan Ibrahim Mosque. In 1912 the mosque was converted into an Orthodox church.

Further to the east is the nearly 5-m (16-ft)-high Byzantine-Venetian town wall, which is surrounded by houses. The fortifications were strong enough to repulse several attempted invasions, but they finally fell in 1645, after 55 days of siege. The Turkish army of Yussuf Pasha had conquered the city.

Othós Kaneváro will take you alongside the Greek-Swedish excavations in **Plateía Ekateríni**. This dig, excavated between 1969 and 1984, provided sensational proof that western Crete was once the centre of Minoan civilisation.

From here, it is a short walk to the eastern harbour with its seven remaining

arsenals (at one time there were 23), its wharves and winter quarters for the galleys.

If you haven't yet had lunch, you may adjourn to one of the many *tavérnes*. Usually these are relatively quiet during the day, but at night you will find them heaving with tourists and locals.

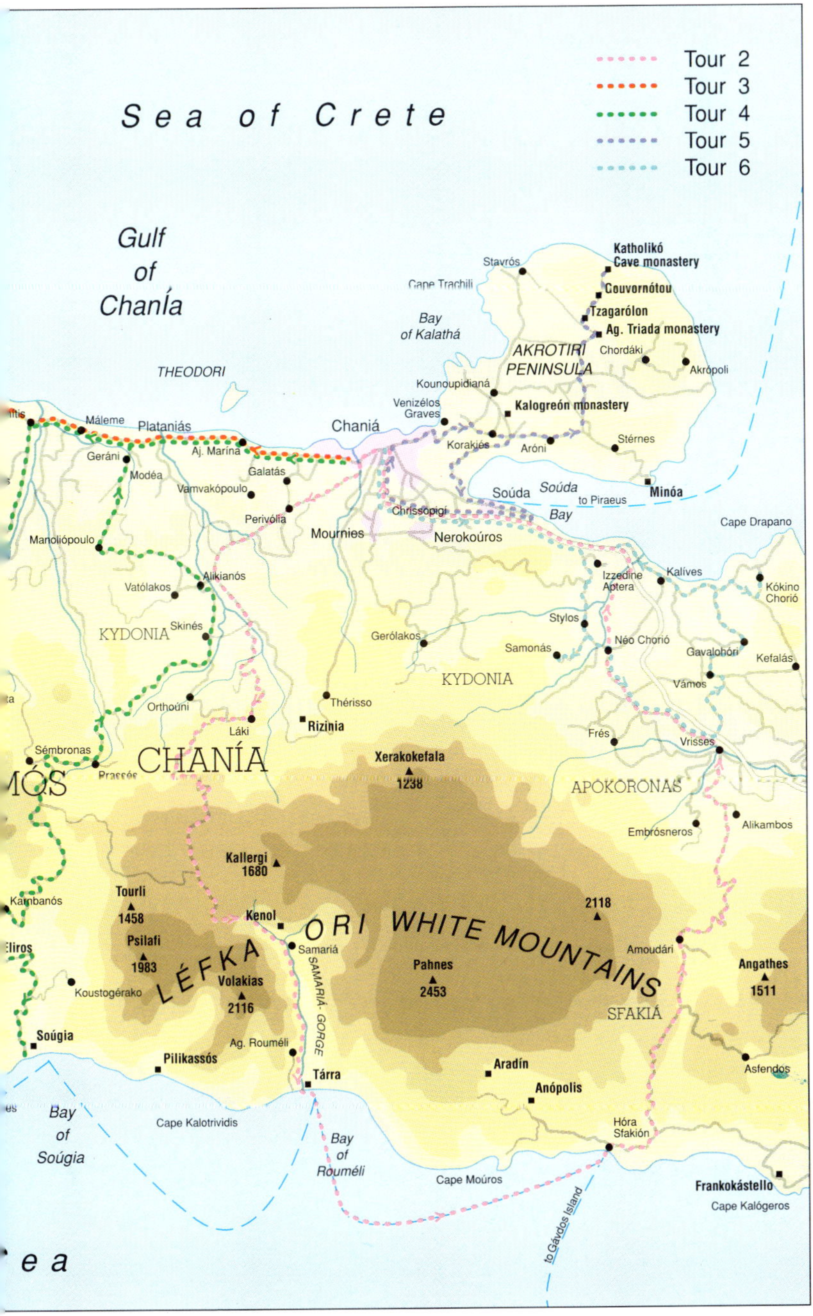

2. In the Mountains of Sfakiá

The Omalós Plateau; Samariá National Park, Europe's longest ravine; the wild coast of Sfakiá; the Askífou Plateau with its wonderful cheese. A day-long trip. **See the map on page 28.**

Located at an elevation of 1,080m (3,543ft), between the districts of Kydonía, Sélino and Sfakiá, the **Omalós Plateau**, with its 25sq km (10sq miles), provides grazing land for numerous flocks of sheep. In addition to grain and potatoes, a variety of herbs thrive here. Inhabited only in summer, the plateau has small hotels, private rooms and several *tavérnes*. During winter months the snow here is a metre deep.

There are several buses leaving daily from the KTEL bus terminal in Chaniá. The route runs via Alikianós, through orange and olive groves and the mountain village of Lákki on to the plateau. The Omalós is surrounded by the peaks of the **Lefka Ori** range, the tallest of which, Páchnes, rises to a height of 2,452m (8,044ft). With its three points of access easily defendable, this plateau was long considered the heart of Cretan resistance. Only twice did Turkish troops manage to advance this far.

Set out on your day's journey as early as possible – preferably the evening before and not during the peak tourist season. Off season and in the early light, these marvellous mountains are seen to their best advantage. The **Tzani Cavern**, approximately 2,500m (2,734yds) long, is to the northeast. In autumn, the *katomerítes*, or lowlanders, come up here to pick the tender *stamnangáthia*, a sort of thorny dandelion plant.

The Omalós Plateau is the starting point for a hike through the longest and most famous (18kms/11 miles) ravine in Europe: the **Samariá Gorge**, in the national park by the same name. The Ancient Greeks believed that this precipitous gorge was the source of the light brought to mortals by the god Apollo. It is open to the public (May to October, 6am–6pm), though sometimes closed due to flooding. The descent begins at the **Xilóskalo** at the end of the asphalt road.

In peak season, up to 2,000 people trek through the ravine every day. Nevertheless, you should not miss this wild mountain landscape, still the natural habitat of the indigenous wild goat, the *krí-krí*; and of eagles, falcons, buzzards and lamb vultures. About halfway through the ravine you will come upon the

In the Lefka Ori

deserted settlement of **Samariá**, once the Venetian Santa Maria and, further down, the church of Osiá María Aegyptía, with its frescoes dating from the 14th century. In 1770, following an uprising in Sfakiá, thousands of women and children sought refuge here. The sheer walls of the ravine, which rise up to 60m (195ft) high, are only 3m (9ft) apart at the narrowest point.

The trail crosses the creek several times and there is a lot of scree on the way, so you should wear sturdy walking shoes for this hike! At kilometre 13 (mile 8), the end of the national park, a welcome sight awaits you: a kiosk selling drinks. Passing the ruins of the old village, you reach the new **Aghiá Rouméli** with its *tavérnes* and pensions. In ancient times this is where Cretan cypress wood – much coveted in the ancient world – was exported to Egypt. Today, small boats provide regular service to Hóra Sfakión, the 'capital' of the region of Sfakiá. From there, the last rural bus to Chaniá (they run every two hours) departs at 7pm.

It is a wild, rugged coastline, with mountains dropping off sharply into the deep blue sea, receding here and there to reveal a tiny cove. The history of Sfakiá is just as wild as the topography, and the people are considered to be the proudest, most freedom-loving and hospitable on the island – but also the sort one would not like to be at odds with. They are also said to be longer-living than other Cretans.

During the Ottoman Occupation, Sfakiá still retained the wealth it had accumulated from sea trade and piracy. The numerous uprisings, however, left it largely impoverished, and it is still the most sparsely populated region on Crete. In 1877, the Turks destroyed **Hóra Sfakión**. Considered to be at 'the end of the world' some 25 years ago, these days the town boasts a large number of *tavérnes,* hotels, pensions and rooms to rent, most of them clustered around the small harbour.

Heading back north, the road passes through the wild **Imvrós Gorge** and the heartland of Sfakiá, the **Askífou Plateau**, at an elevation of 1,730m (5,675ft), surrounded by the tallest peaks of the **Lefka Ori**. Seven settlements overlook the plateau, much like spectators seated in an amphitheatre. The plateau, which provides the only land access to Sfakiá, is a fruit and wine-growing region and the cheese is wonderful. We recommend you give the *sfakianés pítes* with honey a try.

3. Kíssamos: Monasteries, Churches and Beaches

The Goniá Monastery above the sea; a special church in Episkopí; the Chryssoskalítissa Monastery with the legendary 'golden step'; dining under the mulberry trees. A day-long trip, with extensive stretches of unpaved road. See the map on page 28.

The road west to **Kastélli/Kíssamos** passes through ribbon development fringed by stands of bamboo, from which the natives weave baskets, fashion fishing poles and sun roofs, and carve flutes. In Máleme, look out for the sign (on the left) for the spaciously laid-out German military cemetery, the final resting place of 4,465 men.

After Melithiana, take the right fork to Kolimbári with its fish restaurants. Overlooking the sea at the edge of town, you will find the **Goniás Monastery** (closed 12.30–4pm), which was originally built between 1618–34 but has been destroyed and rebuilt numerous times. Inside the church, located in the middle of a courtyard, you will find one of the most important icon collections on Crete. A cannonball in the wall of the apse is just one reminder of the monastery's long and turbulent history.

From Kolimbári, you need to take the old road to Chaniá from which you can reach Episkopí, with its Michaïl Arkángelos Church. Beautifully restored, this church is the only rotunda on Crete, dating back to the 7th, 8th or 10th century.

Michaïl Arkángelos Church in Episkopí

The next stretch on the winding road to Kastélli takes you through a silvery olive grove. Just before Kastélli, not far from where the old and new roads converge, turn up to picturesque **Polirrínia**, a small village built into the side of the mountain. An ancient settlement lay high up on the mountain opposite. There is not much left of it, but the view alone – out over the **Gulf of Kíssamos**, flanked by the peninsulas of Rodopolí and Gramvoúsa – is worth a half-hour climb. (In midsummer, do not attempt this between noon and 6pm!) Otherwise, stop at the advantageously situated taverna in the village.

The route from Kastélli to **Plátanos** is paved; after that, a gravel road weaves its way down to **Falássarna**, the former port of Polirínia, with its glorious beach (unfortunately the greenhouses that have sprung up here detract from the beauty of the surrounding area). There are two small *tavérnes* where you can take a breather.

Continuing south from Plátanos, the road winds high above the sea, leading (unpaved from just beyond Kámbos) through a number of pretty villages bedded in green. In Kefáli, you can turn off for Elafonísi (don't take the earlier turning if you want to avoid an adventurous, and time-consuming, trek along the coast). Though this route (16km/10 miles) is also unpaved, it is relatively easy driving.

Positioned atop a rocky outcrop the **Chryssoskalítissa Monastery**(7am to sunset), to the right of the road when it reaches the coast, is visible from a great distance. The western-most point on Crete, in ancient times this was a place of refuge for the ship-wrecked. A legend tells of 90 steps here, one of them made of gold and invisible to sinners. Hence, the name: Monastery of the Virgin of the Golden Step.

Chryssoskalítissa Monastery

A single nun and a monk inhabit the monastery today, and the explanation given for this surprising arrangement is that only a man is able to hold mass. Actually, this chaste cohabitation is not only common practice in Crete, but it is fully sanctioned by episcopal authority.

Elafonísi, the small island with the white dunes lying just offshore, is perhaps the only island in the world which you reach without the help of bridge or boat – the sea surrounding it is so shallow. And yet it is also here that the *lívas*, the Saharan wind, churns up the highest waves in the Mediterranean. In 1907, such waves took their toll on the *Imperatrice,* which belonged to the Austrian Lloyd shipping line. The victims are buried on the island. On Easter Sunday, 1824, they say, the sea turned red here when 850 women and 40 men were slaughtered by the Egyptian troops of Pasha Ibrahim.

As the summer progresses, the 'mainland' beach gets more and more littered, partly due to illegal camping and partly to outright abuse of the environment. The road back to Chaniá via Kefáli and **Elos** – the Cretan chestnut capital, with its annual Chestnut Festival (third Sunday in October) – takes you through the wild ravine near **Topólia**. Just before reaching Kolimbári you can stop off at **Bárbas Leftéris** in **Kimissianá** for some splendid dining under the mulberry trees – they serve sumptuous Cretan specialities and wine straight from the barrel.

4. To Sélino in the Southwest

A charming drive, crossing the mountains to the south, with time off for a swim. A half-day excursion. See the map on page 28.

You may want to extend this outing to a full day, especially if you decide to stop for a swim. This route appears quite long on the map, but it consists almost entirely of well-paved, wide roads, first west towards Tavronítis, and then south from there towards Paleóhora. The thrill of driving from the north to the south on Crete lies in crossing the mountains to the Libyan Sea. The landscape, cultivated since Minoan days, is characterised by seemingly endless olive groves.

Kándanos, on a slope stretching all the way to Paleóhora, is a village with no charm, the highest rainfall in Crete and a sad history. A commemorative stone in the village square is a tragic reminder of the destruction of the village in 1941 by the German Wehrmacht. The new village, with its post office, police station and shops, has become a centre for surrounding villages.

Paleóhora is a pleasant little town on the southern coast, still unspoilt by mass tourism. Boats ply between here and Hóra Sfakíon, as well as to the tiny island of Gávdos, Calypso's isle and the southernmost point in Europe. There is a sandy beach stretching out to the west of the town, and a more sheltered pebble beach to the east (both are equipped with showers). You will find plenty of hotels, pensions and private rooms here. There are also plenty of fish restaurants on the harbour and at the foot of the ascent to the Fortézza at the southernmost point of the beach, as well as the sophisticated **Fortézza Restaurant**, with its marvellous view of the sea and mountains. The most beautiful hotel in Paleóhora is the old **Libykó** at the entrance to town. Many of the guests come here from the island of Gávdos.

On the road to Soúgia, you can stop for a rest at **Asogirés**, a tiny town in a green valley with several *kafeneía*. Not far away, you can visit the tiny museum in a monastery erected in honour of the '98 holy fathers', the *Aghiï Patéres*. The friendly custodian conducts tours of the church and museum, which contains weapons, clothing, books and pots. Not far from here, you may also seek out the 'miracle

The Church of Aghía Iríni

View of Paleóhora

tree', one of the few evergreen plane trees on Crete. According to legend, the holy fathers in their cave up on the mountain (known as the Cave of Sowé) all died at precisely the same time as Holy Ioánnis O Xénos (John the Foreigner), because they had left him behind on the little island of Gávdos on their way to Crete from Egypt. Here, too, the locals celebrate on 7 October the 'forgotten' saint's name day with a big festival, or *paniyíri*.

On the road to Soúgia, below Teménia, you will find an architectural gem: the **Church of Sotíros Christoú**, with its groin-vaulted dome. Originally a small fishing village on a wide pebble bay, **Soúgia** today is a popular resort and excursion destination. High up on the hill, the Church of **Aghía Iríni** (12th century), with its groin-vaulted dome, has a stunning view of the surrounding landscape.

On the drive back to Chaniá, you can make a stop at the turn-off for the village of **Sémbronas** for some hot food and locally-made wine by the carafe at the **Kafeneíon Sémbronas**.

Roadside message

5. The Akrotíri Peninsula

An array of monasteries; a visit to Bear Cave; the lively little port of Soúda. A morning tour. **See the map on page 28.**

There is more to see than monasteries on the peninsula northeast of Chaniá, though they alone are well worth a trip to this lovely (and strategic) area. Chaniá is expanding rapidly onto the peninsula, but while more and more holiday villages are popping up on the west coast, the east and south, in contrast, are characterised by military zones – NATO bases sealed off from the public. Near Stérnes is Chaniá airport as well as the military airfield.

From Chaniá, drive uphill on the airport road and, once you have attained the heights, stop at the **Venizélos Graves** (signposted). Elefthérios Venizélos was Chaniá's favourite son, scion of one of Greece's most important political families. After his death in Parisian exile in 1936, he was buried here with his son, Sophoklís. With the Lefka Ori towering above it, this park offers one of the loveliest views of the city below. Come in the early morning to hear plainsong drift through the doors of the attendant church and ring through the shady gardens.

British military cemetery near Soúda

A short way past the turning for the graves, turn left for Kopakiez and the **Kalogreón (Moní) Monastery**, a convent with a well-kept courtyard full of flowers, and a place of tranquillity and beauty. The nuns here sell beautiful, handwoven table-cloths.

Back on the main road, follow signs for the airport and thence **Aghía Triada Monastery** (closed 2–5pm), the convent's big brother, which dates back to the beginning of the 17th century. The Renaissance façade is a visual symphony of pink and red – particularly picturesque in the light of the setting sun. Consecrated to the Holy Trinity, the church is situated in the middle of an arcaded courtyard, and the monastic complex contains a collection of valuable icons and other art treasures.

Your route continues via a gravel road up the mountain to the **Gouvernéto Monastery**, the exterior of which greatly resembles a fort. This monastery dates from the 16th century, and the church, with its splendid façade, is consecrated to the All-pure Virgin (*Ee Panagheía*). On 6 and 7 October here, the local residents pour into the courtyard to celebrate a religious festival, or *paniyíri*.

Aghía Triáda Monastery, Akrotíri

A half-hour's walk down the mountain will bring you to the long-abandoned **Katholikó Cave Monastery**, past the **Bear Cave**, which served as a place of worship as early as the late Stone Age.

After first climbing along the opposite side of the Akrotíri Peninsula, the road finally returns to Soúda by way of the airport. At the near end of Soúda Bay, you will come upon a reminder of things past, the British military cemetery which holds 1,527 graves of British soldiers who died defending Crete during World War II.

Soúda is a lively little port, its daily rhythm determined by the departures and arrivals of ferries to and from Piraeus. At 15 kilometres (9 miles) long, Soúda Bay is one of the finest natural harbours in the Mediterranean. For this reason, it has long been valued as a site for naval bases.

A tree-lined road now takes you back to Chaniá but, just before you reach town, there is a boulevard on the left leading to the very beautiful, renovated **convent of Chrissopigí** (The Golden Spring), dating from the 16th–17th century. The fact that candles alone illuminate the church here makes for a very special atmosphere, especially during evening services (*esperinós*).

Home on the Akrotíri Peninsula

6. Yoghourt and Honey

The remains of Aptera; yoghourt and honey in Vrísses; the villages around Vámos. Half-day tour. See the map on page 28.

–Leave Chaniá on the Réthymnon road.–

Signposted off to the right 12km (7½ miles) from Chaniá, on an artificially created plateau, are the ancient remains of **Aptera** (8.30am–3pm, closed Monday). The headland's strategic location is representative of the type of site chosen by the bellicose Dorians: it was impossible for ships to approach Aptera unnoticed. The city, which grew wealthy as a result of maritime trade, reached a pinnacle of influence in the 3rd century BC, but was destroyed by an earthquake in AD700. The site was re-discovered in 1834 by the English traveller Pashley, and later excavated by Italian archaeologists. The harbour lay on the opposite side of the bay, in what today is Maráthi and was called Minoá in antiquity.

The city's name, which means 'wingless', is said to date back to a contest between the Sirens and the Muses. Overcome by grief at their loss, the Sirens tore off their wings and fell into the sea, metamorphosing into the islands which separate Soúda Bay from the open sea. On the drive up the mountain, keep your eyes open for Roman cisterns along the way, as well as for a Turkish **fortress** erected in 1816.

On the road to Stylos (signposted left on the way back to the main road) look for the **Church of Panagheía Serviótissa**, which dates from the 11th–12th century, situated in the middle of an orange grove. It has an octagonal dome which is unique on Crete. **Stylos**, a small village surrounded by greenery, is well-known for its mineral water. From here, the road branches off to Samonás, from which a gravel road leads to one of the island's most beautiful Byzantine churches, **Aghios Nikólaos** (near Kyriakosélia) dating from the 11th–12th century. In **Samonás**, a stop at the small

Almirída and Pláka

From Aptera, a view of the former prison

kafeneíon is a must. Order a Greek coffee or a *tsigouthiá,* Crete's version of *oúzo* (it's strong!), and ask for the key to the church.

Your next stop on this itinerary is the pretty village of **Vríses**, situated beside a stream under mighty plane trees, where you can enjoy fresh home-made yoghourt with honey. Heading out of town in the direction of Chaniá, the road forks off to the right towards Vámos, and winds up the mountain. Halfway up on the left, you will see below you the small, deserted **Karídi Monastery**, which belongs to the wealthy Aghía Triáda Monastery on the Akrotíri Peninsula. The monks' cells have collapsed, and **Aghios Geórgios,** flanked by two mighty walnut trees in the middle of the courtyard, is today just a simple country church.

There are many charming villages clustered around **Vámos**: **Gavalohóri**, which belonged to the Byzantine Gavaládon family, is very pretty with all its restored houses; as are Aspro, Pláka and Kókkino Horió. A natural place for a rest on the way back to Chaniá is **Kalíves**. The little restaurant (*estiatório*) called **Sorbás** is a good bet.

Gavalohóri

Réthymnon

'Réthymnon is a small town… They used to say, in the old days, that its trade was praiseworthy, its shipping flourished and, what is more, that a few good poets and painters were born here.' This is how Pandelís Prevelákis, well-known as a novelist even outside Greece, begins his chronicle of life in Réthymnon, his home town. By way of return, in 1987, a year after the writer's death, the town honoured him with a monument erected in front of the town hall.

Painted entirely in tawny yellows, Réthymnon's old quarter is as picturesque as that of Chaniá. Venetians and Turks built their homes, churches, and mosques here, along with a solid, extensive system of fortifications – meant to be the 'town within a town' – on the hill that juts into the sea. The narrow streets, crowded with shops and restaurants, still bustle with activity.

Up until the 14th century, Réthymnon was no more than a tiny fishing hamlet. However, by the beginning of the 16th century it had grown into a significant town with a population of 10,000. The Greek and Venetian aristocracies divided the power among themselves, and yet the common citizenry here, having acquired wealth from the burgeoning export trade, gained political influence earlier than elsewhere in Europe. In the outlying villages, however,

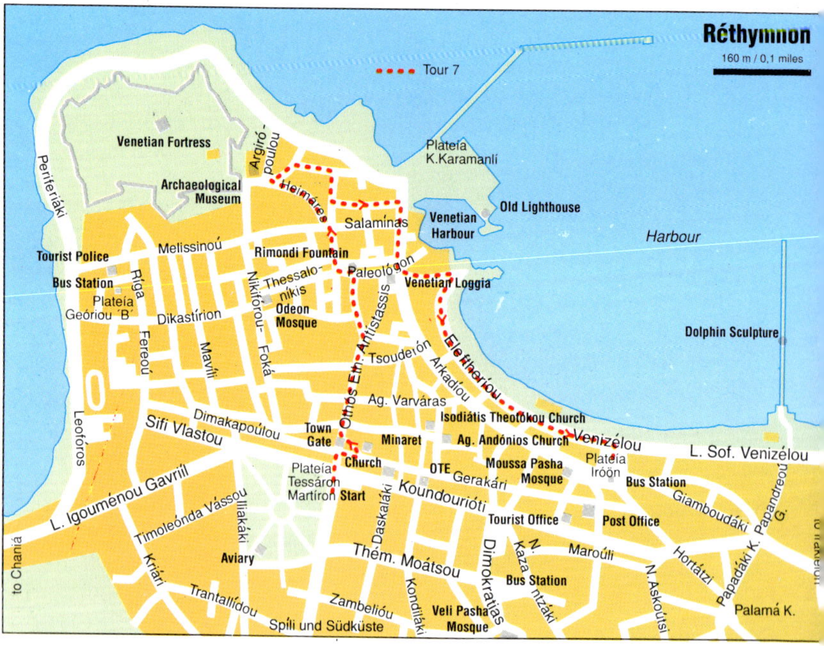

The old harbour of Réthymnon

the peasants found themselves shouldering the double burdens of high taxation along with being forced to contribute their labour to build the town's fortifications.

The Cretan Renaissance flowered at a time when Greece was already under Ottoman domination. It ushered in a unique period of literary excellence in Réthymnon. Yiórgios Chortátzis wrote his masterpiece, the tragedy *Erofíli*, during this period. In 1561, the first Greek intellectual centre since the days of Byzantium was founded here: the Vívi Academy. All this cultural ferment contributed to the town's reputation as a place of scholarship.

Today, Réthymnon is still the capital, trade centre and port of the Nomós of the same name. It is the smallest and most mountainous of Crete's prefectures – dominated as it is by the Psilorítis massif – and the main agricultural products are olives, olive oil, carob and vegetables.

Tourism, however, is beginning to play an important role here, with half of the 20,000 inhabitants drawing their income from the industry. In summer, expect to find the old harbour area packed with visitors, especially during the evenings.

The Old Quarter below Fortézza

7. Réthymnon's Old Quarter

A morning tour of the town, its mosques and churches, streets and alleys full of shops and charming houses; a stop in one of the typical old 'kafeneía'. See the map on page 40.

The starting point for this walk through the town is the elongated central **Plateía Tessáron Martíron**, northeast of the Public Gardens (site of the annual wine festival in July). In 1824, three members of the Turkish aristocracy were executed here. They had been found guilty of the crime of remaining secret Christians despite their public conversion to Islam. The square is named after these martyrs and there is a popular festival held here in their honour every 28 October. A bronze monument commemorates another hero: Kostís Giamboudákis, who detonated the ammunition dump inside the Arkádi Monastery (*see itinerary 11*). Peeping above the square, you will see the minaret of the **Megáli Pórta Mosque**, which is entirely surrounded by buildings and can only be visited by way of the garden at Odós Tombási 27. The **Megáli Pórta**, also called Pórta Guora, is all that remains of the Venetian town wall built to protect Réthymnon from the south. It was the central town gate and is still the entrance to the Old Quarter.

From here, proceed down **Odós Ethnikís Antístaseos**, following a signpost for the Venetian Fort. This street is lined with shops, as well as with Venetian and Turkish houses worthy of leisurely examination. On the left-hand side, diagonally opposite the Odós Tsouderón and set back a bit from the street, you will discover one of the most beautiful Venetian churches on Crete: the renovated **San Francesco**, dating back to the 16th–17th century. Once the heart of an important monastery complex, it is today owned by the University of Crete and used for public events. In the **Plateía Peticháki**, the former **Nerantzes Mosque**, largest of the five mosques

Réthymnon's lighthouse

Neratsé Mosque

still standing of the original eight, has also been converted for secular use. The top of this minaret once afforded visitors a marvellous view out over the roofs of the old quarter to the Fortézza in the north, the beach to the east and all the way to the Psiloritis and Ida Mountains in the southeast, but these days you are not allowed to climb the minaret for safety reasons. The mosque, formerly the Santa Anna Church and topped by three cupolas, is used as a concert hall and music school today. The Venetian **Rimondi Fountain**, installed further down the street in 1629, virtually disappears among the many tables and chairs of the surrounding restaurants and cafés during summer. The water gushes from four lions' heads between four slender columns capped with Corinthian capitals. The Turkish dome-shaped roof was partially destroyed during World War II.

From the fountain, turn the corner and strike up Odós Mesologiou, passing the Catholic church on your right and the Historical and Folk Museum (8am–1pm and 6–8pm, closed Sunday). At the top of the street, turn left to reach the Venetian **Fortézza** (daily 8am to sunset) on the rocky cape in the north, once the site of the ancient city of Ríthimna. The cornerstone for this complex of fortifications was laid in 1573, and the battlements were completed in 1580, the fruits of some 76,800 days of slave labour on the part of the population. The fortress proved too small to accommodate the entire populace as was originally intended and, in 1646, it withstood the Turkish siege for only 30 days. The Turks turned the episcopal seat into the Sultan Ibrahim Mosque (its ruin still stands), and it was here that the German Wehrmacht established a place of execution during World War II. Today, in summer, plays are performed and concerts held on one of the bastions facing the town.

The former prison lying

Megáli Pórta Mosque

below the fortress houses a good **Archaeological Museum** (8am–3pm, closed Monday), which provides generous and attractive exhibition space for finds dating from the Neolithic period to the Byzantine era, including Late Minoan clay sarcophagi, ceramics, jewellery and a collection of coins.

Return to the Catholic church via Odós Cheimares, and retrace your steps to Rimondi Fountain. From here, turn left down Odós Paleóglou to reach the **Venetian Loggia**, once the gathering place of the Venetian aristocracy and now the Archaeological Museum Shop. The harbour, just a few paces further on, was originally built by the Venetians in the 13th century. It has been rebuilt repeatedly since then and, in 1882, a canal was dug to prevent silting due to northerly winds and sea currents. Many older residents can still recall waves lapping up against the restaurants on the seaside promenade.

At the other end of the promenade, near the Plateía Iróön, you will find the **Moussa Pasha Mosque** (the stump of its minaret remaining) which houses the Monument Preservation Board. Above the bus terminal is the

Véli Pasha Mosque with its minaret, the former heart of a *teké*, or Islamic monastery, of which 13 cells have been preserved. Across the street, on **Odós Kountouriói**, you will find refreshments at one of the typical old *kafeneía*, somewhat cheaper than the seafood restaurants on the harbour.

A full day's drive, through the lovely Amári Basin with its orchards and churches. Break the day with a trout lunch. See the map on page 44.

–Leave Réthymnon early on the old Réthymnon–Irákleion road, turning off right for Prasiés a few kilometres out of town.–

During the Venetian-Turkish War, the bard Bunialís of Réthymnon sang the praises of a hilly landscape surrounded by mountains – the Amári Basin – calling it 'Paradise', and Mount Kédros (1,777m/5,830ft), at its western edge the 'site of 100 springs'.

Flanked by Mount Psiloritis to the east, the **Amári Basin** stretches 25km (15½ miles) to the south, with 40 villages on its slopes, 400–500m (1,300–1,600ft) high. The basin is divided by Mount Sámitos (1,014m/3,327ft). Amári fruit is often praised, particularly the cherries and apples which thrive here, but also the table olives. This is the loveliest region on Crete and the most abundant in both water and Byzantine churches.

The first stop is the **Church of Panagheía Myrtiótissa** in **Prasiés**, with remains of frescoes dating back to the 14th century. There are still a few Venetian houses extant in the village – evidence of former affluence.

At Apóstóli, stop for a drink at the taverna on the right-hand side of the road. Here, you may be lucky enough to bump into John Neonakis, the hand behind the sculptures of the village square. Ask him to reveal the mythical/political significance of his figures. Beyond Apóstoli the road divides, the two forks circling opposite sides of the basin. Take the right-hand one to the large, scenic mountain village of **Méronas** which, back in 1878, was the seat of the revolutionary general assembly. Further up the mountain is the triple-naved **Panagheía Basilica** – its 14th-century frescoes only partially uncovered. Dating back to the 15th century, when painted panels began replacing frescoes, the wooden icon in the **Panagheía Odigítria** is one of the oldest on Crete. The road now winds its

Apóstoli in the Amári Basin

Vrontíssi Monastery

way to **Elenes** and the cherry-growing village of **Gerakári**, the starting point of an optional hike up **Mount Kédros**. The road to Ano and Káto Méros takes you down the **Platys river valley**.

Continuing towards the southeast via Platános and Kamares (turn right at the junction outside Nithavris), the next stop on your itinerary is the monastery church of **Valsamónerou**, 3km (2 miles) south of Vorízia. The church contains frescoes which span several centuries – these are among the most significant works of Byzantine art on the island. Among the saints consecrated by the church is Saint Phanoúrios, the patron saint of lost objects or causes. To gain admission to the church, ask in Vorízia (‘*Pou íneh o fílakas tou monastiríou?*’ – ‘Where is the caretaker of the monastery?’).

A bit further south, 3km (2 miles) this side of Zarós, watch for the signpost to the next monastery on the southern slope of Mount Psiloritis. **Moní Vrontíssi** (550m/1,804ft), surrounded by mighty, 2,000-year-old plane trees, was first documented in the year 1400. In the double-naved church in the middle of the spacious courtyard, you can admire the beautifully restored 14th-century frescoes and wooden icons which come from Valsamónerou Monastery.

Zarós, a large, green mountain village further south, at the foot of Mount Psiloritis, is known for its trout farms. Here you should have a late lunch at one of the trout restaurants situated above the town. Head back north via Kamáres, to Vizári. A gravel road opposite the post office takes you to the well-preserved foundations of the former **episcopal basilica**, which dates from the 7th century. According to legend, this is where, until 1821, Antifandís – a participant in Napoleon's Egyptian campaign – trained the troops so dreaded by the Turks.

The road left up to the one-time ‘capital’ of **Amári** is lined with pines, eucalyptus trees and grain fields. A walk up to the cemetery is worth the spectacular view of Psiloritis.

Before returning to Réthymnon, take one last detour to the hamlet of **Thrónos**: the mosaics of the former episcopal basilica, located in front of the small, single-naved **Church of the Panagheía Throniótissa** (with its 15th-century frescoes), bear witness to its days as a diocesan town.

9. Préveli Monastery and Frankokástello

A Late Minoan necropolis; Préveli Monastery; Fort Frankokástello, with its 'shadow warriors'; and a refreshing swim. A full day's excursion. See the map on page 44.

Your route today consists almost entirely of well-maintained roads, and you should have time for some leisurely bathing along the way. Leave Réthymnon on the Chaniá road, quickly turning off for Spili. Ten kilometres (6 miles) south of Réthymnon, off to the right just before Arméni, is a **Late Minoan necropolis** (8.30am–3pm, closed Monday and in winter), one of the largest such burial sites in Europe. A shepherd discovered the first grave here in the late 1960s; today, 64 rock chambers have been excavated, containing sarcophagi, earthenware, jewellery, tools and seals.

Twenty-three kilometres (14 miles) out of Réthymnon, there is a turn to the right, to the monastery of Moní Préveli, which leads through one of the most beautiful ravines in Crete, **Kourtaliótiko Gorge**. The north wind blows here, frequently and fiercely, producing the rattling sound – *koúrtala* – for which the area is named. The stream flowing through the ravine is the Megalopótamos. Popular tradition attributes its origins to Saint Nikólaos who, like Moses, caused water to gush forth from stones.

At the first village after the gorge, branch left following signs first for Plakiás, and then Préveli Monastery, passing, on the left a disused stone bridge, surrounded by rushes and osiers, from where you can climb up to the 16th–17th-century **Káto Monastery** (consecrated to John the Baptist) further up the hill.

The road continues to climb to the **Préveli Monastery** (closed 2–4pm) which dates back to the 17th century. 'It is the paradise of Crete', wrote the English cartographer Spratt during the last century, 'at an extremely happily selected site conducive to withdrawing from the cares and responsibilities of life.'

The monastery's affluence was based on those classical treasures of Crete – olives, honey, and flocks of goats and sheep. Many Orthodox Christians bequeathed their possessions to the monastery to prevent them from falling into the hands of the Turks – so that its vast estates eventually reached from the Libyan to the Cretan Sea. During World War II it was from here that Allied soldiers were evacuated to Egypt, after which the Germans looted the monastery. Only

Préveli Monastery

Káto Préveli Monastery

the silver cross containing the splinter of the True Cross was returned, because the German aircraft with this precious freight on board was simply unable to get off the ground. Nearly all of the 20 cells here are unoccupied today: this lovely monastery with its view over the southern sea has become, for the most part, a sightseers' destination. Annually, on 8 May, the church's patron saint, Ioánnis O Theológos (John the Evangelist), is honoured by a festival. At one time the celebrations called for the sacrifice of cattle, a holdover from the rites of antiquity.

From the monastery, regain the road to Plakias and thence to Mýrthios and Selliá. Through a harsh, karstic landscape – rarely charming, almost chilly – high above the southern coast, the road continues through the villages of Káto and Ano Rodákino (Lower and Upper Peach), down onto the plain to the growing resort of **Frankokástello** with its flat sandy beach and choice of several *tavérnes* in which to have a late lunch.

Built by the Venetians in 1371 as a refuge for the local population, the fort was also used against the resistance fighter Sfakiás. The rectangular outer walls with their towers at each corner are still standing. In 1828, 700 freedom fighters lost their lives here. The monument erected to commemorate their heroism is dedicated to their general, Hadzimihális. No adequate scientific explanation has ever been found for a mysterious phenomenon involving the so-called phantoms of these warriors, the *drossoulítes,* or 'dew men', which are said to appear in the first light of dawn here in the latter half of May. Apparently the mirage occurs only when atmospheric conditions are right.

Just beyond the fort is the Byzantine church of **Aghios Nikítas** decorated with 14th-century frescoes, built on the foundations of an early Christian basilica. Below the building, at the foot of a bluff, you will find another sandy beach. It only remains to wish you *'Kaló bányo'* (have a good swim).

Fort Frankokástello

10. The Soul of Crete

Argiroúpolis, a large mountain village among cypresses and olive trees; the high Kallikrátis Plateau; dinner at a cosy taverna. **A half day's trip. See the map on page 44.**

The old road from Réthymnon to Chaniá threads its way through a silvery landscape blanketed with olive trees, and hamlets off the beaten track. Turn left for Episkopí, where the road begins to climb. Only 260m (853ft) above the sea and not far from it lies the former silver mining town of **Argiroúpolis**, a large mountain village on the site of the ancient settlement of Láppa (ignore the signpost to the site itself for the time being). Once a mighty city of 10,000 people, Láppa experienced its heyday when Crete was a Roman province. Today, you can pick out ruined fragments of Láppa's structures incorporated into the walls of the village houses or scattered in front of churches.

During Minoan times, all of Crete must have been forested as densely as the environs of Agiroúpolis. The Venetian church belfries are the last reminders of the days when the town was still an important centre of Venetian Crete. During the Turkish era, its status declined to that of a *gaïthourópolis*, or 'Donkey Town'. But at an assembly in 1878 this town is where the question of union with Greece was resolved.

Eight kilometres (5 miles) higher up the mountain lies tiny **Myriokéfala** – its new church of the **Panagheía Odigítria** (follow the road looping round the village) containing parts of the old church and marvellous frescoes dating back to the 11th and 12th centuries. The interior of the church resembles a defensive fortress. On 7 and 8 September, as many as 15,000 people throng here to the festivities honouring the Virgin.

From here, double back to Argiroúpolis and follow the sign to Láppa (left just below the village). Lush and green, it is irrigated by the same cataract which supplies Réthymnon with drinking water.

View of Argiroúpolis

A quiet spot in Argiroúpolis

The plane trees, particularly tall here, banana groves, poplars, and nut and fig trees – and, especially, the water – make this place a popular destination for summer outings. Try one of the *tavérnes* (closed in winter) for a bite to eat.

Continue past the site for the next stretch of your journey through **Gyparis Gulch** to **Asigoniá**, or 'Revolutionaries' Nook' as the Turks called the village. The lyrics of a popular song run: 'I told you, Mother, I cannot bear the Turks and cannot be a slave. So give me my gun and my silver knife, so that I can go to Asigoniá…' It is a large village on a mountainside dotted with walnut trees and home to many flocks of sheep. On St George's Day, 23 April or, when if it falls during Lent, on the Tuesday after Easter, the shepherds drive their sheep into the village, where the animals are blessed, milked and the milk distributed to the people.

The 12km (7½ miles) of bad gravel road signposted from here up to the small **Plateau of Kallikrátis** (760m/2,522ft) may be a bit tedious, but what magic once you reach the top. The soul of Crete is surely to be found in its mountains, and in those who inhabit their peaks. Of the 400 families which used to live up here – except in winter – only 80 remain. There are a few *kafeneía* where visitors will find a good meal. On 15 August, the village, whose men are considered the handsomest on the island, fills with people for a big *paniyíri*. During the winter, on the other hand, when the inhabitants move down to their winter quarters in Kapsodássos, Kallikrátis is totally deserted.

From here you can either retrace your steps or go via Episkopí to the small freshwater **Lake of Kournás**, or proceed via the gravel road to Askífou and Vrísses. In the village of **Kournás** – not located on the lake – there is a small *tavérna*, I Kalí Kardiá, on the main road (on the side towards the lake), where you will find hearty, delicious food. During the winter, the place is particularly cosy with its roaring, iron stove. From the resort of Georgioúpolis, take the national highway back to Chaniá.

The Lake of Kournás

11. Margarítes and Arkádi

The potters' village of Margarítes and the Monastery of Arkádi. A half-day excursion. See the map on page 44.

The first stop is the **Arsaníou Monastery**, 12km (7½ miles) from Réthymnon off the old road to Irákleion via Pérama. Inhabited by only a couple of monks, it is like so many Greek monasteries. Destroyed many times throughout history, there is little left here except a few beautiful icons in the monastery museum. An old drawing gives an impression of how spacious the monastery complex must once have been. The ancient city of Agrion is believed to have been located near here.

Just after Cháni Alexándrou, the road forks off to **Margarítes**, one of Crete's four historic pottery centres. It was from here that the master craftsmen, all organised into guilds, used to swarm out over the island during the summer, selling their wares in the towns along their way. In 1928 half the population still lived off the production of unglazed pottery. Legend tells of a queen in the ancient city of Eléftherna nearby, who was so enchanted by the location of the town that she donated her jewellery towards the founding of the village.

As you wander through the village, stop to look in the former monastery church of Agios Ioánnis Prodrómos. Above the village, you can still inspect the remains of the old firing kilns. Young potters are now hoping to carry on the ancient traditions. Look out for the large *pithoi*, made in Crete since Minoan times.

The road continues (4km/2 miles) up the mountain to **Eléftherna** perched on a jutting nose of rock. Along with Láppa, Eléftherna was one of the mightiest cities in Roman Crete and continued to be important right up to the Byzantine era, after which it was de-

The monastery church of Arkádi

Arkádi Monastery

stroyed by the Saracens. The most striking remains are the 6m-(20ft-) high cisterns.

From Eléftherna, the next 8km (5 mile) stretch of road takes you to the most legendary of all Cretan monasteries, **Moní Arkádi** (dawn to dusk). At an elevation of 500m (1,640ft), the monastery is located 23km (14 miles) southwest of Réthymnon amidst grain fields and tall pine trees. The Venetian-Cretan stone façade displays the full palette of Mediterranean colours: assorted pinks, delicate yellows, beige and deep ochre.

On 9 November 1866, after a brutal day of fighting against the 150,000 Ottoman soldiers who were besieging the monastery, the 1,000 Orthodox Christians within the walls, unwilling to submit to the Turks, blew themselves up. There were 114 survivors, and the Ottoman casualties numbered 1,500 dead or wounded. As a result of the Arkádi tragedy, funds were raised throughout Europe in support of the Cretan struggle. The monastery that stands at Arkádi today was erected in the 16th–17th century. Shot marks and sword cuts can still be seen on the door of the refectory. The ossuary, beside the car park, is a grim reminder of the events of 1866.

Leave the monastery by the tarmacked road to Amnátos (from behind the complex), which leads back to Réthymnon.

Potter in Margarítes

12. Mt Ida, Zeus's Birthplace

Churches, shepherds and sheep; the cave where Zeus was born. A day's drive to Irákleion. **See the map on page 44.**

From Réthymnon, follow the old road via Plataniás and Pérama, turn off to Garázo and climb up to **Axós**, tucked into the Psiloritis range and at one time the place where travellers journeying between east and west Crete usually broke their journey. With all the shops here selling the usual tourist tat, it is hard to believe that this is where the Minoans retreated in order to escape the advancing hordes of Dorians. Later, the Dorians took the city anyway, fortified it and built an acropolis a bit further up. Axós remained a wealthy and powerful town up until Byzantine times, when the population moved and founded Anóghia.

At a fork in the road in the middle of town you will discover the distinctive **Aghía Iríni Church**, with its groin-vaulted cupola and badly deteriorated 14th–15th-century frescoes. The frescoes dating from the same period are worth seeing in the **Aghios Ioánnis Church** located in the cemetery at the eastern end of the village.

Despite the numbers of visitors it receives, the large, populous village of **Anóghia**, a few kilometres on, is still a beautiful place, known throughout Greece for its fine musicians. The *lyra* player and singer Psarantónis, brother of the widely revered singer, Níkos Xiloúris, who died in 1980, and Ludovíkos, whose repertoire consists of old love songs and laments from his village, are both native Anóghians.

Anóghia has a heroic history of rebellion as well. Destroyed twice by the Turks, in 1821 and 1866, Anóghia was razed to the ground and all its men were executed by the Germans in 1944. Owing to its remote location, Greek traditions and age-old customs are exceptionally well preserved here, along with a distinctive Dorian dialect.

Aghía Iríni Church

Leaving Anóghia, turn off for the Ida Cave (signposted Idéon Andron) situated at an elevation of 1,400 metres (4,593ft), just above the practically circular **Nída Plateau**. The road there (21km/13 miles, only three-quarters of it paved) makes its way through barren, mountainous terrain, past a number of *mitáta* – the shepherds' round, unplastered huts, which bear an interesting resemblance to Minoan burial vaults – and *stroúnga*, round walled enclosures where the sheep are milked and shorn. The earlier part of this route offers some far-reaching views of the north coast.

The Nída Plateau

Eventually, you will reach the most recent in a long series of inns and *tavérnes* that have served pilgrims drawn to the nearby **Ida Cave** since the Bronze Age. Leave your vehicle outside the *tavérna*, and walk up to the cave (turn sharp right just above the *tavérna*), an easy 10-minute climb along track. A place of worship from the Stone Age until well into the early Christian era, the cave merits a visit on account of its mythical associations rather than for what there is to see. It was here that Zeus, the father of the Greek gods, was believed to have been born. Every nine years, the great King Mínos came here to receive from the god himself the laws and regulations which provided the foundation for Mínos's wise rule. Today developers are thinking of promoting winter sports activities here.

After lunching at the taverna (beautiful views of the plateau to the rear), return to Anóghia and proceed along the old road to Irákleion, visiting the remains of three Minoan manor houses (signposted) in **Tílisos** on the way.

Sunny colours prevail

Irákleion

Irákleion is the largest and most important city, economically, on Crete. With over a fifth of the island's population living here in what is the fourth largest city in Greece, Irákleion is rapidly turning into an urban jungle, the 'Athens of Crete', as detractors call it. Besides becoming the Cretan capital in 1972, Irákleion is also the administrative capital and the trade centre for the seven districts of the Nomós. Irákleion has a population of 120,000. This is where most of the charter flights land, and the majority of Crete's million or more summer visitors stop off here at least once during their stay.

All this crowding produces quite a hustle and bustle, especially in summer. But Irákleion lacks the Venetian-Turkish flair of Chaniá or Réthymnon and has far fewer beautiful old buildings. Despite its shortcomings, however, Irákleion is a city with a certain cosmopolitan dash, a trading city with a long tradition. The growth in tourism since the 1970s has given rise to a renovation programme for the old quarter of town but, unfortunately, very little of historical value has been left standing.

Irákleion's past is as turbulent as that of Crete. Under the Arabs, Rabdh el-Khandak, as they called it, had the dubious distinction of containing the biggest pirates' lair and slave market in the Eastern Mediterranean. In the process of recapturing Crete for Byzantium,

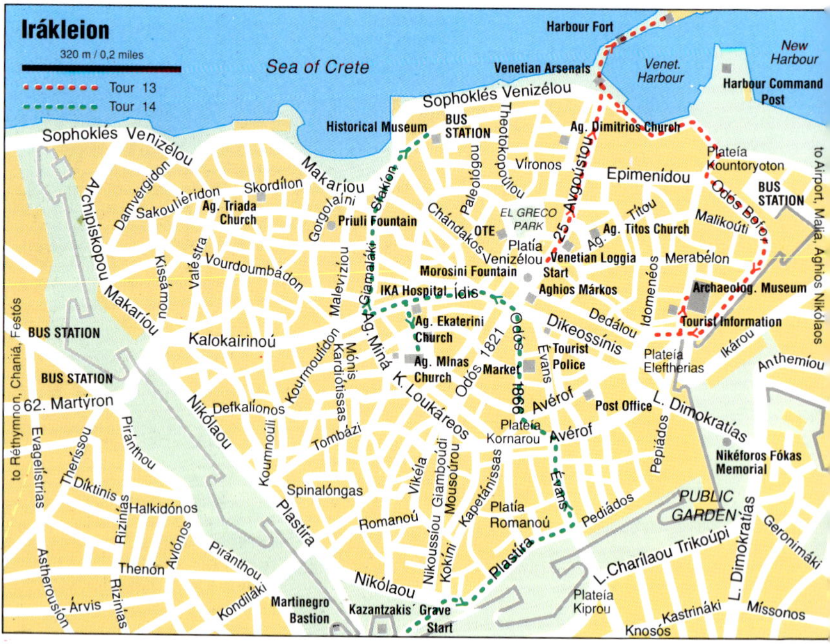

Irákleion harbour

Nikifóros Fokás, at the head of the siege force, had the heads of prisoners catapulted into the beleaguered city. Finally, in 961, he razed the city to the ground, had the Arab population killed or enslaved, bestowing upon what was left of the town the name 'Chántaka'. After a brief Genoese interlude on Crete, the Venetians finally seized the island in 1210, turning 'Chántaka' into 'Candia', and frequently calling the entire island the 'Isola di Candia'. In the 15th century, the school of painting belonging to the monastery of Aghía Ekateríni of Mount Sinai became an intellectual centre and the flagship of the Cretan Renaissance.

During the 16th century, the mightiest fortifications in the Mediterranean were built around Candia. In 1699, after a long siege, Turks marched into the city. One final cataclysm in the saga of Greek resistance, on 25 August 1898, caused the major powers to declare Crete's autonomy. World War II ended seven months earlier in Irákleion, thanks to 50 partisans who managed to trick the German forces into believing they were a superior force numbering several thousand.

In the streets of Irákleion

13. Walking through 'Candia'

A morning tour of Irákleion's Old Quarter covering the Arab and Byzantine city of Candia: the Aghios Márkos Basilica, Rocca del Mare (the Venetian fort) and the Archaeological Museum. See the map on page 56.

Begin with breakfast on **Plateía E Venizélou**, in the heart of the city. With its numerous cafés and restaurants, it is a popular meeting place, and not only for Irákleion's foreign guests. Once the grain market, today the square is a pedestrian zone. The beautiful Venetian

The Harbour

Morosini Fountain, with its four lions, presented to the public in 1628, is the symbol of the city. An **Aqueduct**, over 15km (9 miles) long, was meant to provide Candia with water from Arhánes. The crumbling reliefs on the outer walls depict stories from ancient Greek mythology, including Zeus's abduction of the Phoenician king's daughter, Europa. The church with three naves facing the square is the **Aghios Márkos Basilica**, the former San Marco's, consecrated in 1239 and the seat of the Latin bishops during the Venetian occupation. Under the crescent moon of Islam, the church was converted into the Defterdar Mosque and its campanile torn down. The beautiful interior, with its

Venetian lion, a past relic

Theotokópoulos Exhibition in the Aghios Márkos Basilica

wood-panelled naves, is a venue for city cultural events today.

From the square, head down **Odós 25 Augoústou** (25 August Street), passing on your right the **loggia**. After its destruction by earthquake, the building remained a ruin until the end of the World War II. Today, it is Irákleion's city hall.

Just past the loggia, in a small square set back on the right-hand side, is the attractive **Aghios Títos Church**, which served believers of several faiths before becoming an Orthodox sanctuary in 1924. The skull of Saint Títos (Titus) was returned here in 1966 from its sojourn in Venice. Alas, it is not on display. Continuing down Odós 25 Avgoústou – the site of the last Cretan bloodshed at the hands of the Turks – you head towards the Venetian harbour.

Irákleion back street

This street has long been the city's main commercial artery. Most of Irákleion's streets are now dominated by modern buildings, but there are still enough old façades to convey a hint of the city's former splendour. Today, despite its rich history, the street is characterised by banks and shipping and travel agencies. It is also packed with car hire firms and a good place to shop around if you want to hire a car.

The Venetian harbour of Irákleion lacks the unity and charm of those at Chaniá and Réthymnon. Located right on the heavily-travelled shoreline drive, it is a moorage for fishing boats. The only reminder of Venetian and Byzantine glories past is the renovated fort, **Rocca del Mare**, which still has its Turkish name, 'Koúles' and is one of the most beautiful Venetian forts on the Mediterranean. The open upper floor, with its stumpy minaret, is now a summer venue of dramatic performances and concerts. You can have a coffee while admiring the Koúles and the sea at the Marina coffee house, right on the harbour.

From the harbour, climb to **Odós Bofor** (on which the Marin hotel is situated) inside the city walls. Follow the road with the sea on your left to get to sprawling **Plateía Eleftherías**. Until 1917, the eastern city gate, Aghios Geórgios, was here – also known as Lazaréto, because the street to the 'plague house' led through it. Today, the gate has been replaced with a bust of Irákleion's great literary lion, Níkos Kazantzákis, author of *Zorba the Greek*, *Report to Greco* and *The Last Temptation of Christ*.

Tucked away to the right as you enter the square is the **Archaeological Museum** (Tuesday to Sunday 8am–7pm; and Monday 12.30–7pm; 8am –5pm and 12.30–5pm respectively in

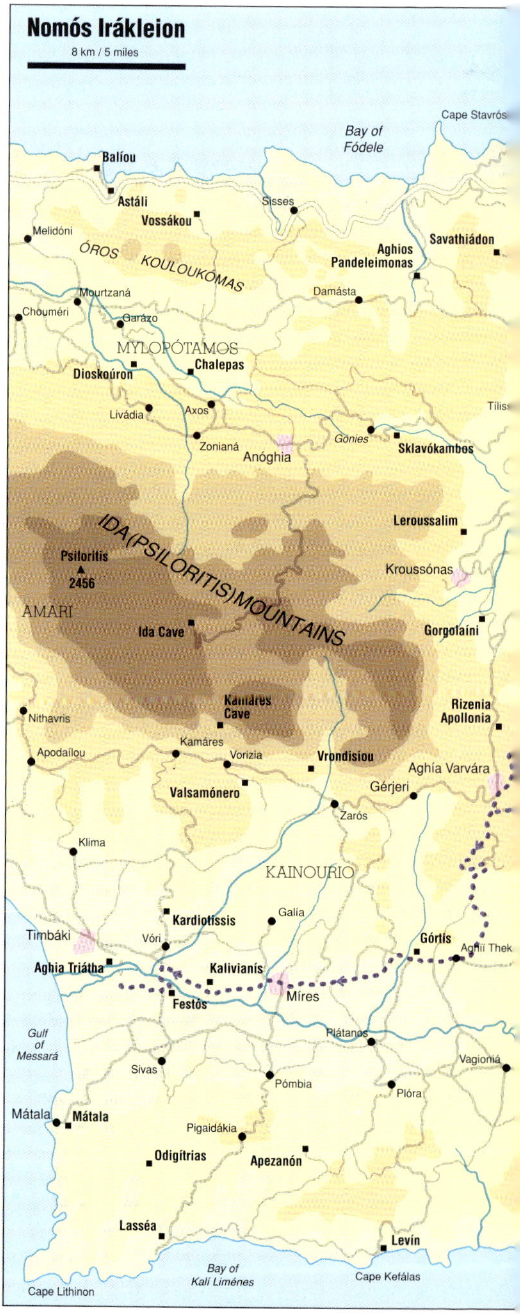

winter) founded in 1878. There are two floors of spectacular finds from 5,500 years of Cretan history. Particularly notable are finds from the Minoan excavations. For a proper understanding of Minoan culture, there is no substitute for a visit to this excellent museum.

Immediately opposite the entrance to the museum, you will find the Tourist Office (Monday to Friday 8.30am–2.30pm) where you can pick up a free map of Irákleion, a list of Crete's hotels and a bus timetable.

14. Venetian Ramparts

A morning tour of the quarter in which the Venetians built their palaces; a view of the 'Slumbering Zeus'; the impressive fortress of Michele Sanmicheli; churches and museums; followed by lunch on the seafront. See the map on page 56.

The inspiring view from the **Martinengo Bastion** should put you in the right frame of mind to begin your second tour of Irákleion. The best vantage point is at the southern point of the fortification walls, where you will find the **grave of Níkos Kazantzákis**, probably Greece's best known author (the grave is signposted left off Nikolau Plastira). The epitaph under the simple wooden cross was written by the novelist, and mirrors his philosophy: it translates: 'I hope for nothing, I fear nothing, I am free.'

From here, Mount Yoúchtas (811m/2,661ft) rises to the south like a slumbering Zeus, reclining in full battle gear, his helmet and profile silhouetted against the sky. Turning your back on the mountain, you will be looking over the fortress wall of **Michele Sanmicheli**. Over 3km (2 miles) long and up to 60m (196ft) thick, it encloses about half a square kilometer (quarter of a square mile) of land. All the men from the surrounding area between the ages of 14 and 60 were enlisted for one week of compulsory labour per year in the building of the fortress. The bastions, housing artillery casements, consisted of several storeys, all connected by tunnels 15–20m (50–65ft) deep. The old access points to the city – the Pórta Chaniá to the west, the Koméno Bendéni to the southwest, the Kenoúria Pórta to the southeast and the Tris Kamáres to the east – are still in use, although not all of the city gates are still standing.

Turkish pump house in Irákleion

From the bastion, return down Nikolaou Plastira to Kenoúria Porta and turn left into Avenue Evans to reach (off to the left) **Plateía Kornárou,** the setting not only of the oldest existing Venetian fountain (executed by Zuanne Bambo, with a headless Roman statue from Ierápetra) and the **Turkish pump house** – which is used as a *kafeneíon* today – but, since 1981, also of the sculpture of Erotókritos and Aretoússa, the star-crossed lovers of the Cretan national epic, *Erotókritos,* which was written by Vitzéntzos Kornáros.

From the square, proceed past the Turkish pump house to **Odós**

The two churches of Aghios Minás

1866, whose name commemorates the uprising at the Arkádi Monastery. This is the place to buy fruit, cheeses and hot snacks, as well as the usual handicrafts.

At the end of the bazaar, turn left and, following the road round, look out for a small passage on the left (Odós Agii Deka) leading to Plateía Aghía Ekaterínis, unofficially known as the Square of Churches.

The former church of **Aghía Ekateríni** belonged to the famous **St Catharine's Monastery** on Mount Sinai, and was once the heart of the Cretan Renaissance movement. This austere building with its barrel vaulting and cupola, a mixture of Venetian and Islamic architecture, is well preserved. Today it houses the **Icon Museum**. The most important holdings here are the panels executed by Michaïl Damaskinós.

In the same square, you will also find the relatively new **Aghios Minás Church**, tangible proof of the continuity of Greek sacred architecture. Completed in 1895, as the archiepiscopal cathedral, it accommodates 8,000 people. Crete has had its own archbishop since 1967, directly responsible to the Greek Orthodox Patriarch in Constantinople. The **Little Aghios Minás Church**, a two-room chapel dating back to the 15th–16th century, is tiny and modest by comparison, but lavishly furnished with a marvellous iconostasis, and picture-panelled walls with typical Cretan carvings and icons by Geórgios Kastrofilakas.

From the square, return down Odós 'Agii Déka, cross Odós Kalokairinoú, turn left and then right again into Odós 1770. Follow Odós 1770 as it winds down to the **seafront**. Turning right along the boardwalk, you come to the **Historical and Folklore Museum**, featuring the library and study of Níkos Kazantzákis, photographs of the Battle of Crete and the battle-scarred city of Irákleion, prints of old Candia and a collection of traditional costumes.

If you are foot-weary and hungry, adjourn to Ippokambos, which serves good food at reasonable prices and is a favourite choice of the locals.

15. Potters and Mountain Villages

A trip through the environs of Irákleion; a potters' village; market day in a mountain village; relaxing under shady plane trees. A full day tour. **See the map on page 60.**

Throughout Crete, if you drive into the more remote regions you will find winding roads, often of poor quality, and no infrastructure of tourist services. Twenty-three kilometres (14 miles) south of Irákleion, you will come to the **Monastery (Moní) of Angaráthou**. At an elevation of nearly 400m (1,312ft), idyllically situated above hills covered with vineyards, this is one of the oldest monasteries on Crete. It played an important role both in the struggle against the Turks and as a centre of intellectual activity. In former times, there was always water, wine, bread and olives deposited in a niche in the flower-filled courtyard, ready to be served to visiting travellers. Today, this tradition continues in the *trápeza,* or refectory. The monastery church possesses a 'miraculous' icon of John the Baptist. During a Turkish attack in 1896, the bullets of a Turkish soldier bounced off it, blinding the man; smoke and noise then filled the air and the Turks took to their heels. That, at least, is how the monks tell the story.

After looping around via Vóni, you will arrive in the village of **Thrapsanó**, the pottery centre of the Nomós Irákleion. As late as the 1960s, Thrapsanó potters organised in guilds fanned out from here to other parts of the island – mainly to fire the characteristic, man-sized storage vessels, or *píthi*, used in Minoan times. In the intervening decades, however, the potters have settled down, and their *píthi*, rarely used now to store oil and wine, serve mainly as giant planters. In addition to the village's several small workshops, there is a potters' co-operative south of town from which the terracotta ceramics – still turned by hand as they have been for thousands of years – are exported throughout Europe. The clay, which comes from the surrounding area, is repeatedly sieved to obtain as high a standard of purity as possible. After the first watering and kneading, the clay is kept under cloth until used. The axles of the wheels are set in the ground, and the wheels themselves are just above the ground. A boy down in a ditch turns the wheel while the master forms the pot on the wheel above.

The pottery in Thrapsanó

From here it is not far to **Kastélli/Pediáda**. Despite the town's proximity to the tourist 'strongholds' of Chersónissos, Amnissós and Mália, this

The area around the Epanosífi Monastery

has remained a sleepy little one-mule place. Just a stone's throw away, above the village of Xidás, keep your eyes open for a narrow track through the fields. There isn't so much as a sign to indicate that this was once the location of Lyttos, one of the mightiest cities of ancient Crete, its port being present-day Chersónisos. The excavations are modest, but the location on the northwestern slope of the Díkti Mountain range and the view are spectacular. Owing to its protected location, Lyttos was not fortified – a rarity, and a luxury in the bellicose ancient world.

The agricultural centre of the area is the large mountain village of **Arkalohóri**, southwest of Kastélli. Here, Saturday is market day, and the place bustles with people buying merchandise. Arkalohóri's reputation is based on the Minoan findings discovered here in 1932 in the Profítis Ilías Cave. According to the late archaeologist Spyridon Marinátos, there is reason to believe that this is the original Díkti Cave, the reputed 'birthplace' of Zeus.

In the beautiful old mountain village of **Ano Viánnos** on the road to Ierápetra, you can soak up pure village atmosphere sitting outside a *kafeneíon* under 220-year-old plane trees. This is where Ioánnis Kondilákis was born in 1861. His novel *Patoúchas* captures with great charm the way of life in a Cretan village. Outside the town, look for a simple monument to the 400 men, women and children from surrounding villages shot and burned here in 1943 by German soldiers. Down below, beside the Bay of Keratókambos, is the small village of **Arvi**, famous for its small, fragrant bananas.

The road now heads north via Pírgos on the edge of the Messará Plain to the **Epanosífi Monastery**, still home to 30 monks. It is a so-called idiorhythmic monastery, where each monk keeps house for himself and property is private rather than communal. In front of the church, the large stone table surrounded by stone benches is where the first wine casks are opened and the first *tsigouthiá* tasted every 3 November, at the religious festival honouring Saint George.

The wine-growers' association in the village of **Pezá** on the way back to Irákleion produces some of the finest wine on the island.

16. Arhánes, Vathípetro and Mt Yoúchtas

A small town worth visiting not only for its Minoan excavations; a Minoan wine-growing estate with a marvellous view; up Mount Yoúchtas to the birthplace of Cretan Zeus. A morning tour. See the map on page 60.

At the foot of **Mount Yoúchtas**, in the middle of Crete's richest wine-growing region, you will find the cheerful town of **Arhánes** (from Irákleion, follow the Knossós road, then fork right 11km/7 miles from Irákleion). The town gleams – with its *arhontiká spitia* (manor houses), its beautiful old *kafeneía* with their high windows and its covered sidewalks, all radiating bourgeois affluence. With its three naves and detached bell tower, the Venetian **Panagheía Church** on the main street is worth seeing.

Arhánes became internationally famous when excavations proved the site was a major centre of Minoan culture. The complex unearthed in the former Turkish Quarter, the *tourkoyitoniá* (to the left of the main road as you enter the town from Irákleion), indicates that the village was quite a splendid town in antiquity.

The **Fourní Necropolis** (8am to noon; call tourist office for summer opening hours) is along a rough road signposted as you enter town (park your vehicle and go on foot – it isn't far). The necropolis is where a truly sensational find was made: the unplundered grave of a priestess or princess, the upper, domed section of which had been used for centuries by shepherds as a shelter. Searching the surrounding area, scientists turned up one of the largest Bronze-Age necropolises ever found, with numerous domed tombs.

Yet there was an even more exciting and still controversial find in store: the discovery of a Minoan temple in **Anemóspilia** (also signposted from the centre of Arhánes) on the northern slope of Mount Yoúchtas. Here a youth was apparently sacrificed in place of a bull to avert a natural disaster, perhaps an earthquake. If archaeologist Ioánnis Sakellarákis' theories are correct, this represents the only such occurrence on Crete. Despite publication in such periodicals as *National Geographic*, the sacrifice is still in dispute. In Arhánes you can also visit a museum housing finds from these archaeological sites (9am–2.30pm, closed Tuesday).

The Minoan wine-growing estate in **Vathípetro** (8am to noon; call the tourist office for summer opening hours), 8km (5 miles) south of Arhánes is reached via a gravel road leading up and

Excavation in Tílissos

Wayside scene near Epanosífi

to the left after the turn-off to Yoúchtas (an easy drive in spite of the bad road surface). It is a small estate and its open terrain affords a magnificent view of the vine-covered, hilly landscape. The excavated sites include a wine press, a weaving shop and a pottery.

Making your way back to Arhánes, climb the gravel road (5km/3 miles) to the mythical **Mount Yoúchtas** (811m/2,661ft), preferably on foot, if it is not too warm. According to the myth, this is the location of the grave of Cretan Zeus who, unlike Olympian Zeus, was immortal, and annually resurrected from the dead. The **Summit Chapel**, to which people in the surrounding villages throng for a *paniyíri* on 6 August, is not consecrated to the prophet Elijah (who, like Zeus, is responsible for the weather) as is customary, but to the Transfiguration of Christ, *Metamórphosis Christoú.* After all, like Zeus, Christ died and rose again.

Pause for thought

17. Knossós and Mália

An outing for archaeology enthusiasts. A half-day excursion. See the map on page 60 and archaeological plan on page 70.

Both Knossós and Mália are easy to reach by rural bus. The best season to visit the palaces, especially **Knossós** (daily 8am–7pm, 8am–3.30pm in winter), the most popular tourist sight on Crete, is between November and March, when the busloads of visitors are absent. From Irákleion, the road to Knossós is clearly signposted.

The turn-of-the-century English historian Arthur Evans, who originally travelled to Crete in search of clay tablets etched with hieroglyphics, excavated an area of 20,000sq m (23,920 sq yd). In the years since, scholars have come to doubt Evans's assumption that Knossós was the location of King Mínos's palace. It seems more likely that the site was a trade centre governed by a priestess-queen, although there will be no hard and fast evidence for this premise as long as the 'Minoan' script remains undeciphered. One thing remains undisputed, however: the Greek archaeologist who first located the giant *píthi* here, Mínos Kalokerinós, and Evans, who reconstructed the site, did succeed in discovering the most important city of ancient Crete.

A model in the Archaeological Museum in Irákleion will give you a good idea of what things looked like here during the Late Palatial Period, from 1600–1450BC. The two- to four-storey buildings were connected in irregular fashion and grouped around a large inner courtyard surrounded by open passageways, with red-painted cypress trunks as supports and large frescoes on the walls. Evans had parts of buildings and columns reconstructed out of reinforced concrete – which met with a great deal of criticism. Note the representation of the double axe and the bull's horns: the

Unearthed pithoi

The Palace of Knossós

attributes of the Great Goddess, prevalent motifs in Asia Minor during the Late Stone Age and, in fact, as early as the Early Stone Age in Europe. An earlier palace here was destroyed by a natural disaster in 1700BC; the newer one in around 1450BC. Nevertheless, Knossós flourished during the Classical Period, remaining one of the island's major urban centres until the Roman era. In AD827, the Arabs dealt its death blow.

The coast road to **Mália** – the second oldest ancient palace excavated on Crete – takes you through the oldest cultivated landscape in Europe. However, these days, mass tourism has taken its toll here, and the admittedly fine beach is lined with luxury hotels, bars and restaurants. The most extreme example of overdevelopment is **Chersónisos** with its fashionable shops.

The **Minoan port town** of Mália (8.30am–3pm, closed Monday) lies east of the modern resort (tucked into the end of the long beach), grouped around an unfortified palace. The complex dates back to the Late Palatial Period. The architecture at this site is much simpler than that at Knossós.

The wife of Mínos

Knossós Palace

30 m

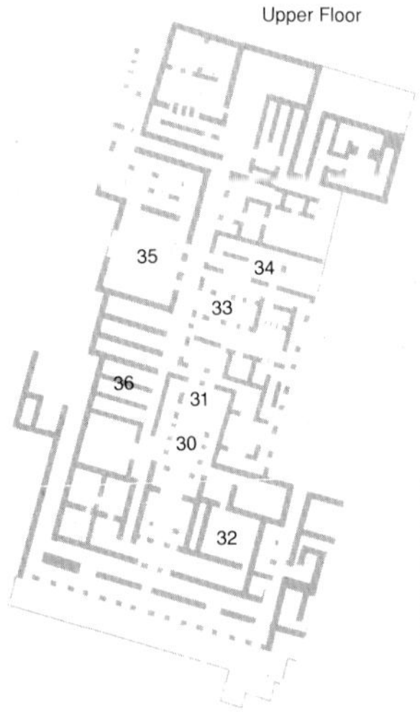

1 Main Entrance
2 Procession Corridor
3 Southwest Entrance
4 South Corridor
5 South Entrance
6 Shrine of the Double Axes
7 Bathtub
8 Central Courtyard
9 Throne Hall
10 Three-part Sanctuary
11 Pillar Crypt
12 Staircase to Upper Floor
13 Propylaeum
14 Archive
15 Sanctuary with the "Miniature Frescp"
16 Room with the "Crocus Plucker"
17 Bathroom
18 Storehouse
19 North Entrance
20 Hall of Pillars
21 Bull Relief
22 Workshops
23 Giant Pithoi
24 Engraver's Workshop
25 Hall of the Double Axes
26 Bathtub
27 Toilet
28 Staircase
29 Lily prince fresco
30 Main Staircase
31 Upper Propylaeum
32 Loggia
33 Hall of Pillars
34 Staircase to Central Courtyard
35 Store Administration Office
36 Storerooms

18. A Roman Metropolis

From the centre of Crete to the agricultural Mesará Plain: more ancient ruins, churches and palaces. A half-day excursion.

Just this side of **Aghía Varvára**, on the road to Míres and Festós, there is a small church perched on a rock. This is believed to mark the centre of Crete, the exact middle of the island. Once you have skirted the foothills of the Psiloritis range and climbed the **Vourvoulítis Pass**, you have a clear view of the **Messará Plain**. Forty kilometres (25 miles) long and 8–12km (5–7 miles) wide, and cut off from the sea by the **Asteroúsia Mountains** to the south, this is Crete's largest agricultural area. Here, too, you will find greenhouses popping up like mushrooms.

This side of Górtis, also called Górtina, you will come to the village of **Aghiï Théka**, named for 10 martyred bishops tortured to death here during the 3rd century. In the gorgeous quarter

The fertile Messará Plain

around the **Aghiï Théka Basilica**, dating back to the 13th–14th century, you may well come across the remains of the odd Roman column in the middle of the street.

The ruins of the Roman capital of **Górtis** (8am–5pm) spread out on both sides of the road. Scholars inform us that it was once inhabited by 200,000 people, the most important city on the island for a good 1,000 years until it was devastated by the advancing Arabs during the 9th century. The fenced-in area to the north of the road contains the **ruins** of the Church of St Títos, once a mighty,

Aghía Triátha

domed basilica with three naves, as well as of the Agorá and the Market. The **stone tablets** along the northern wall of the Odeon document the acclaimed municipal laws of Górtis, which earned Crete the reputation in the ancient world of being particularly sophisticated in the realm of jurisprudence.

South of the road, in the middle of an olive grove, is the town's centre of power, the **Praetorium**, the palace district of the Roman praetor. Like the remains of the Temple of Apollon Pythios, the site is fenced in but accessible to view. The excavations here draw considerably fewer visitors, which makes for a tranquil atmosphere.

Back on the road, head on through **Míres**, the true agricultural centre of the Messará Plain. The Minoan **Palace of Festós**, (8am–5pm in winter; 8am–6pm in summer) on top of a hill, affords a marvellous

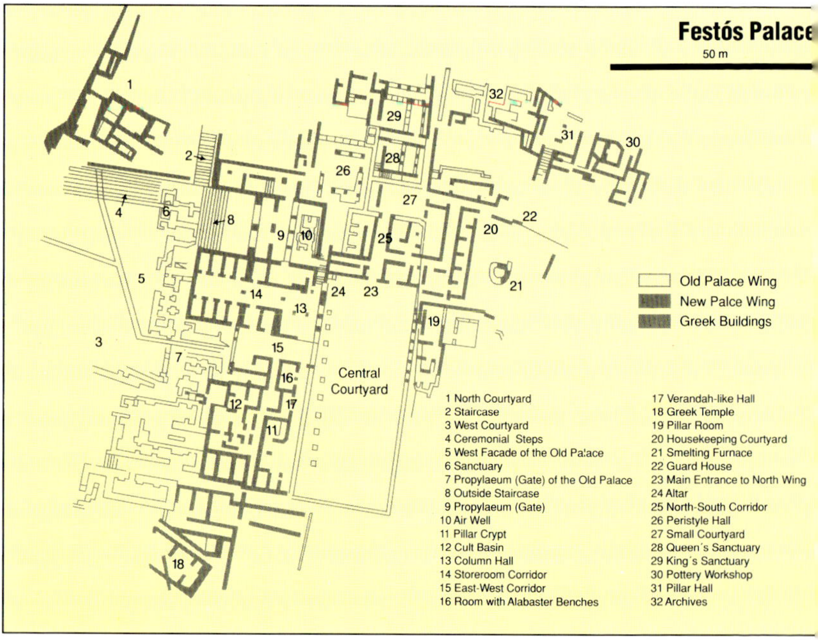

view out over the Messará Plain, with its extensive olive groves, vineyards and fields of grain, across to the Psiloritis range, and the villages dotting the opposite slopes. The layout of the palace is similar to that at Knossós, but on a much smaller scale, with the various wings grouped around a central courtyard, procession-ways and a 20-m (65-ft) long monumental staircase. The famous *discus,* or disk, of Festós, a clay disc with hieroglyphic inscriptions, is probably the most significant find – though its purpose has not yet been firmly established.

During Minoan times, a cobbled road led to the so-called **Villa of Aghía Triátha**, 3km (2 miles) away, above the Libyan Sea. Here, the major finds were valuable frescoes, as well as an entire archive of clay tablets. The complex has been dated to before 1550BC, but there are still questions about its significance: it was clearly designed according to a scheme different from that of the palaces.

For the drive back to Iráklеion, we recommend the scenic detour (via the turn-off for the east this side of Aghía Varvára) through the mountain village of **Aghios Thomás**. Grouped around bizarre boulders, only a few of the town's former 38 churches are still

View of the Palace of Festós

standing: the restored Byzantine **Aghios Thomás Church** in the market square is particularly worth seeing.

If you would like a short rest before driving on, try one of the *kafeneía* along the main road. Spring visitors should try to time their visit with the annual celebration of St Thomas's Day, on the first Sunday after Easter.

Lassíthi

In 1889, Sfakiotes from Crete's 'Wild West' founded a settlement on the Gulf of Mirabéllo, naming it after the small Byzantine church nearby, Aghios Nikólaos; today called simply 'Aghios'. Since the early 1960s, Aghios Nikólaos has been the scene of an incredible tourist boom. Although the city has neither an airport nor a large harbour and its beaches are tiny, the centre, with its beautiful old tile-roofed houses surrounding the small harbour and the freshwater lake, has undeniable flair.

Orientation is simple, everything is easy to locate and the northern coast has not been destroyed. The city lives off tourism and, from April to October, this is even more obvious than in other Cretan towns. During winter, things are quieter, and most of the restaurants and many of the shops close.

Although Aghios Nikólaos is a young city, the urban site itself and the surrounding countryside have a history which stretches back far in time. In antiquity, a Dorian port was located further inland here, on the Goulá Heights. In 1206, Enrico Pescatore claimed the spot for Genoa, founding the Castello di Mirabello, the 'Fort with the Pretty View', atop the ruins of the ancient city situated on the low foothills. Henceforth, this fort lent its name to the entire region, taking on the Cretanised form of 'Merambéllo'. In 1905, Aghios Nikólaos became the capital of the Nomós Lassíthi, one of the most fertile areas of the island, containing the governmental districts of Merambéllo, Lassíthi, Ierápetra and Sitía. Once a year, on Saint Nicholas's Day, of course, Aghios Nikólaos honours its patron saint. On this occasion, local celebrities, the Bishop of Pétra and numerous visitors gather around the Church of Aghios Nikólaos, one of the oldest and most beautiful churches on Crete.

Lassíthi Plateau

19. Picturesque Aghios Nikólaos

An introductory stroll round the town and the harbour, including a dip into the Archaeological Museum, followed by a visit to the Church of Aghios Nikólaos, with its painted Byzantine interior. **See the map on page 76.**

This tour begins at the small, 64-m (210-ft) deep Lake Voulisméni – also called Xepatoméni, 'the bottomless one' – which is the social hub of Aghios Nikólaos for locals and visitors alike. In 1903, the lake emitted sulphuric vapours, which nourished the theory that it is connected somehow to the Santorini volcano. The Voulisméni is surrounded by restaurants where you may not be able to enjoy the full gamut of Cretan cuisine, but you will certainly find a hearty breakfast (the full English version is a speciality) to set you up for

Aghios Nikólaos harbour

the day. According to myth, this is where the goddesses Athena and Vritómartis, the Cretan Artemis, bathed. At one time the lake was famous for its 'sweet water' but it is now regarded as salty.

Heading up **Odós Paleológou** (uphill from the bridge at the neck of the lake), you will come to the **Archaeological Museum** (8.30am–3pm, closed Monday), situated in a section of town named after the original Arab settlers, **Arápika**. The exhibits are arranged in eight rooms; they include Minoan objects found in the surrounding area, including wine goblets, weapons, double axes, sarcophagi and idols. From this elevation, you will also have a beautiful view of the coast stretching northwards towards Eloúnda and Pláka; of the little island of Aghiï Pándes, a preserve of the wild goat, or *krí-krí* ; and of the tiny island called Mikrónisí, to the east of the Aghios Nilólaos.

View of Aghios Nikólaos

Return down the hill and turn right, anticlockwise round the lake, and climb up the wooden walkway cut into the cliff. At the top, turn left down N. Plastira and stop at The Café, a pleasant bar with a balcony, for a cooling drink and a view over the lake.

At the bottom of N. Plastira, turn right for **Plateía E Venizélou**, a busy square where a monument in greenery in the middle of the square honours 400 people shot by German forces to the southwest of the city in 1943. At the corner of Odós 28 Octovríou and Pl. El. Venizélou there is a traditional *kafeneíon* serving the Greek delicacy sweet *loukoumádes*. From here, Odós S Venizélou will take you down to the KTEL bus terminal (signposted), with its simple *souvláki tavérnes*, currently a bit removed from the bustle but unlikely to be so for long in view of the new marina. This is the place to pick up local buses for tours of the island. Not far from here, below the road to Sitía, you will find the largest beach close to the city, the **Almyrós**, which has an extensive range of water-sport activities.

From here follow the shoreline from the beach back to the city (keeping the sea on your right). The breakwater, consisting of concrete pilings spaced a metre apart, will give you an idea of how rough the sea gets here in winter. **Kitroplateiá Bay,** where the *kitra*, the citrus fruit, used to be loaded, is now used as a beach. The walk continues to the harbour, where once a week a steamer drops anchor before returning to its home port of Piraeus via the Cycladic islands, Kárpathos and Rhodes. There are also regular boats from here direct to Piraeus, and this is where touts drum up custom for pleasure cruises to the island of Spinalónga just north of Aghios Nikólaos.

Crossing the bridge over the canal you come to the tourist information office (the best place to enquire about bike and car-hire and excursions) and the **Folklore Museum** (April to October, 9.30am–1pm, closed Saturday), with its attractive collection of traditional costumes, hand-woven textiles and Byzantine icons. Odós 28 Oktovríou then leads to **Odós Iróön Politechníou**, which in turn ends at **Kefáli Hill**, where the Genoese erected their **Castello di Mirabéllo**.

The city's oldest anchorage is north of the road to Eloúnda, in the small Aghios Nikólaos Cove. Not far away, in the grounds of the Minos Palace Hotel, is the church after which the city was

Lake Voulisméni

named – built no later than the 10th century and one of the oldest churches on Crete. Unfortunately, the painted interior, the only one of its kind on the island, has been only partially preserved. Dating back to the period of controversy regarding the worship of images (726–843), and the representation of human beings in church art, the wall decoration here represents some of the rarest Byzantine painting in all of Greece. Later, the ornamental frescoes were partially painted over. You can ask for the key at the reception desk of the Minos Palace Hotel.

20. The Lassíthi Plateau

The fertile highlands between the majestic peaks of the Díkti Mountains; a monastery, and an exemplary folklore museum; the Díkti Cave. A whole day's tour. See the map on page 80.

The obvious springboard for the Lassíthi Plateau is **Neápoli**, or 'New City', 12km (7 miles) from Aghios Nikólaos, off the main road to Irákleion. Laying out the broad streets and large squares here, Pasha Adosídis intended to make this town the capital of the newly-created Nomós Lassíthi. This is also the town where, several centuries earlier, in 1409, a son of poor peasants set out into the world. This native son with humble beginnings was later to become Pope Alexander V. Above Neápolis is the site of ancient Dríros, of which only a few ruins remain.

From here, the road winds its way up, slope by slope, through Amigdáli and Zénia, and the scenery gets greener as you go. On the left rise the bare, majestic peaks of the Díkti range. In summer, the tourists set out at about 11am, so we recommend you get an early start from Aghios Nikólaos or drive up to the plateau the previous afternoon.

Once the granary of the Venetians, the **Lassíthi Plateau,** at an elevation of over 800m (5,625ft), is one of the most fertile regions on Crete due to an abundance of water derived from melting winter snows. Practically everything grows here except citrus and olive trees: grain, vegetables, fruit, lentils and chick peas. The farmers here complain bitterly about their competitors, the greenhouse-owners, who flood the market with cheap vegetables. Since 1890, the windmills here, with their canvas sails, have served to pump up water from the limestone; and to an extent, they still do. More and more, however, the mills are being replaced by diesel pumps.

The peaks of the **Díkti Mountains** embrace the 60sq km (21 sq miles) plain which, from above, resembles a hand-woven carpet. It is patterned with soft, wavy lines and its 21 villages are all situated along the outer edges of the plain so as not to waste so much as a square metre of the fertile earth. These villages are inhabited by over 5,000 people, though many of the younger Lassithiotes work in the coastal tourist trade in summer.

They say that here, in the Greek Switzerland, the climate is so healthy that the people can do without doctors. The eight passages up to the plateau used to be so narrow that two people found it difficult to squeeze past each other and thus these access routes were easy to defend. It is no wonder that

The way up to the Díkti Cave

Street trader

this natural fortress was at the heart of many revolts and constituted a safe haven throughout history. Because of the heavy resistance here, the Venetians deemed it a 'thorn in the heart of Venice' and so prohibited all cultivation and pastoral agriculture in Lassíthi for two centuries. Violators had one leg amputated. Later, however, Venetian engineers constructed irrigation systems which are still operational today.

We begin our clockwise tour of the plateau at the **Kristallénias Monastery**, where the *paniyíri* of the Panagheía Church is celebrated on 15 August annually, the 'name day' of the Virgin.

In **Aghios Geórgios**, the **folklore museum**, organised in an exemplary manner and housed in an old, windowless building, documents the life of an earlier century, showing household furnishings, crafts and agricultural implements.

The main attraction of this area is undoubtedly the **Díkti Cave** (Dikteo Andro), situated above Psychró. This is the cave where the Great Goddess was worshipped from as early as 2000BC on. Later, the Greeks established the cave as the birthplace of the almighty father of their gods, Zeus. In the myth, Cronos ate all his newborn children out of fear that when they grew up they would oust him from power. When it was time for her to bear Zeus, Cronos's wife Rhea outwitted her tyrannical cannibal of a husband, saving the infant by giving birth in a cave. Crete's Díkti and Ida Caves both lay claim to be this mythic site, though the dispute has been settled by calling one the birthplace and the other the nursery of the god. The hike up to the entrance takes 15 minutes, and seems a lot

Harvest time

longer in high summer, so there are 'donkey taxis' available.

Below Ambelos, with its stone mills, which is one of the points of access to the plateau, there is a path from Kerá up to the **Karfí**, a peak visible from far and wide and a Minoan shrine and sanctuary. The hike up takes about an hour and a half; you should follow the

red markings and as usual try and avoid the middle of the day in high season when the sun is at its most merciless. Only the foundations of the settlement are left, but while enjoying the view from this vantage point you can imagine what those Cretan recluses of yesteryear must have felt like, living up here.

21. Fresh Fish and Palm Trees

A remote natural landscape; the quiet town of Sitía; authentic Cretan cuisine and delicious fish; the palm grove of Váï; the Toploú Monastery. A whole day's excursion. Pack a bathing costume. **See the map on page 80.**

The road from Aghios Nikólaos to Sitía runs high along rugged coast, lined with oleander, broom, pines and cypress trees, occasionally dipping down to the beaches (one of the best of which is below the road at Istro, a few kilometres south of Aghios Nikólaos). Though winding, the road is well paved.

Shortly before **Chamézi**, look for the Minoan **'Oval' House** perched just above the road on the right. Experts are still unsure as to whether this was a sacred building or a dwelling.

As a springboard for tours of eastern Crete, **Sitía** (population: 9,000) is a duller but quieter alternative to crowded Aghios Nikólaos. The houses are set into the steep western shore of Sitía Bay, and the narrow, little-travelled streets are connected by stairs.

Some finds from the area of the city indicate a Minoan past. Looming over Sitía, the Venetian-Turkish **Kazárma Fortress** is an impressive sight. Today it is used for theatre performances and concerts. Sitía is a stolid little provincial town with limited tourism as yet, and small hotels and boarding houses.

The **Archaeological Museum** (8.30am–3pm, closed Monday), with finds from eastern Crete, is signposted on the road to Ierápetra. Down in the harbour, you will find one restaurant after another facing **Plateía Venizélou**. If you are looking for something really 'authentic', try **Kalí Kardía** (the 'Good Heart'), at 20 G Odós Foundalídou (parallel to the harbour, two blocks in), a *kafeneíon/tavérna*, with good, plain food. The **Klimatriá Tavern**,

Harbour and Kazárma Fortress

Palm trees in Váï

with its pretty garden, situated just above the road to Ierápetra, is also recommended.

Eastern Crete consists of hill country. Barely 800m (2,625ft) high, barren and a delicate shade of yellow, the region is reminiscent of African landscapes. The houses in this area have flat roofs, offering the wind, which can be quite brisk at times, less resistance.

From Sitía take the beach road to Palékastro, turning left to **Tóploú Monastery** (9am–1pm and 2–6pm) after some 20km (12 miles). The monastery, prefaced by a line of windmills, looms up like a defensive fort amidst the barren wasteland. Consecrated to the Panagheía Akrotirianí, it was a place of refuge and a centre of uprisings during the Turkish Occupation. During World War II, the Germans shot the abbot here when they discovered a secret radio transmitter in the monastery.

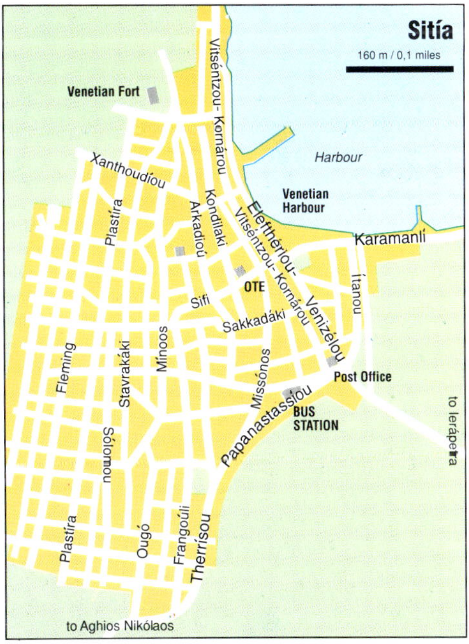

The most beautiful icon in the church is the one portraying the Panagheía Amólinton, the Immaculate Virgin Mary.

From the monastery, continue along the road to the palm grove and justly popular beach at **Váï**. Palm trees grow at

The Minoan 'Palace' at Káto Zákros

only five places on the island. Outlawed during the time of Pythagoras as a pagan symbol of victory, the palm was still used to decorate temples and, even today, churches. On the beach at Váï, tourism has arrived in earnest but it remains a pleasant place in which to while away the hottest part of the afternoon.

Palékastro's offshore peninsula is the easternmost point on Crete. Two kilometres (1½ miles) below the town, beside the good beach, excavation work on one of the most important Minoan ports has been underway since the turn of the century. If the afternoon is fading and you are feeling hungry, take the gravel road leading there – it cannot be paved due to the ancient remains which may still lie beneath the surface – to the fish *tavérna*, **Ee Chióna.** The breezes and the fish are both exceptionally fresh. Lucullus, the Roman gourmet, praised the fish from Palékastro, claiming it to be the finest anywhere.

Alternatively, if you still have several hours before sunset, take the windy drive through karstic landscape to **Káto Zákros,** where archaeologists have unearthed the smallest Minoan palace found to date. Above the extremely fertile land along the Zákros River where the palace lies, you will discover the mouth of the glorious Zákros Canyon – dubbed the 'Valley of the Dead' after the cave-tombs found here. The town's restaurants and the pebble beach are good reasons to spend some time here.

Toplоú Monastery

22. Dorian Idyll

Lató Etéra, ancient Dorian city; the village of Kritsá, with an especially beautiful church; the Katharó Plateau, far from the madding crowd. A half day's trip. **See the map on page 80.**

– There are several kafeneía where you can stop for refreshment on this tour, but it is still a good idea to pack a small picnic. Hikers will want to equip themselves with sturdy shoes, sun hats and adequate water for climbing during summer. –

This side of Kritsá, look for the gravel road turning off to **Lató Etéra.** This is the site of the best-preserved Cretan city dating back to the 1st millennium BC. High up, easy to defend and not visible from the sea, all the Dorian cities have enchanting views. This one owes its name to Lató, a goddess worshipped in this area. Laid out in terraces, the excavated city includes numerous private dwellings, workshops, temples, an *agorá*, or public market-place, a city gate and a splendid staircase.

Kritsá, a majestic village 11km (7 miles) from Aghios Nikólaos, has expanded up a slope at the foot of steep cliffs. It is now one of the largest villages on Crete. The church, surrounded by cypress trees at the entrance to the village, **Panagheía Kyrá**, consecrated to the Virgin, has three naves and supporting pillars. Its three apses and cupola date back to the 13th-14th century. In no other church on Crete are so many frescoes so well preserved as here. It is worth buying an illustrated guide book which describes the church's architecture and holdings from the shop next door, since it is forbidden to take photographs inside the church.

From Kritsá, follow the gravel road for 16km (10 miles) up to the summer home of the villagers, the **Katharó Plateau** (1,100m/3,609ft) an abundant source of potatoes, vegetables and vines in summer but often snowed under in winter. Keep your eyes open as you pass several kermes oaks and you will probably see goats clambering around in them!

This road takes you to another world, far from the bustle of summer tourism, a landscape full of tranquillity and simplicity towered over by **Mount Lázaros** (2,085m/6,562ft), one of the tallest peak in the Díkti range. This is an ideal area for hiking.

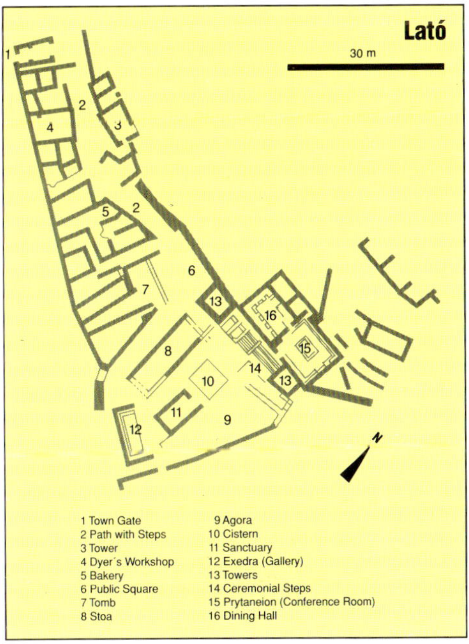

Fresh squid coming up

23. Minoan Gourniá

A perched monastery with a breathtaking view; the Minoan city of Gourniá; the city of Ierápetra. A half-day tour.

On the road to the town of Sitía, 7km (4 miles) on the other side of Kaló Horió ('Good Village'), there is a turn-off to the right onto a steep gravel road (6km/4 miles) leading up to the **Moní (Monastery of) Faneroménis**, which clings to the cliff like a fortress. Few tourists bother to make the climb up here, so the welcome one receives is genuinely warm. A monk will show you round. Don't miss the cave church (accessible from the roof), consecrated to the Panagheía Kímissis, the Assumption of the Virgin Mary (a donation to church funds expected). On 15 August, the day when the Dormition or Assumption of the Virgin is celebrated throughout Greece, there is a celebration here in honour of the Virgin. After your tour, relax over home-made biscuits and coffee in the garden.

Back on the coast road, continue to the Minoan city of **Gourniá** situated in a broad delta, at the foot of a low, gently sloping hill directly above the sea. It is the only Minoan city to have been fully excavated. It consisted of houses, crowded together along narrow

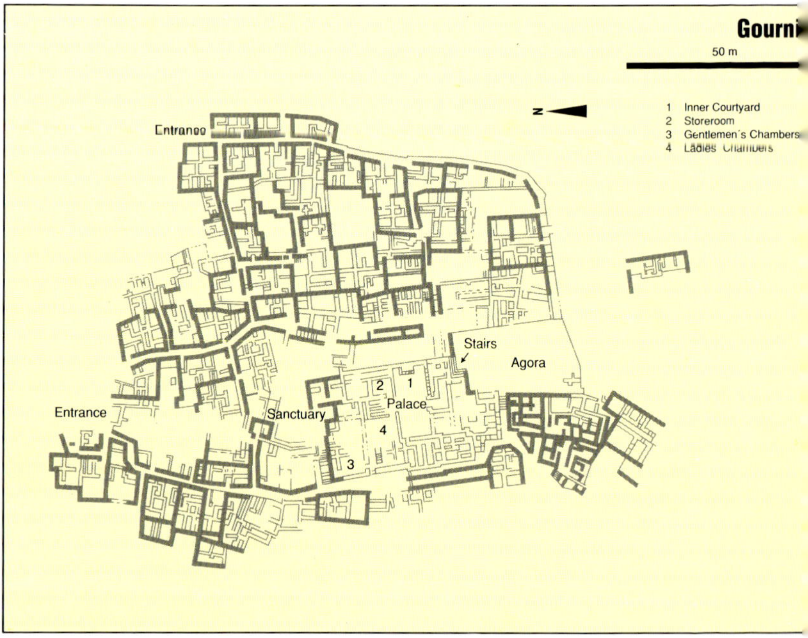

Gourniá, the excavated mountain city

alleyways, with workshops and supply rooms on the ground floors and living quarters in the upper storeys. Gourniá had its heyday during the period of the New Palaces between 1600 and 1450BC.

Beyond Pachiá Ammos ('Fat Sand') turn right for the road to Ierápetra and pass through the island's 'wasp waist', the narrowest place on Crete. Half-way there, in Episkopí, look (on the right) for the 11th–12th-century **Church of Aghios Geórgios and Harálambos** with its two naves and cupola.

Descending to the sea, you reach **Ierápetra** – with its 8,600 inhabitants, the major town of the southern coast. It lies on a fertile plain, which has been disfigured by the arrival of endless, plastic greenhouses. Ierápetra has the lowest average rainfall and the highest number of sunny days in Europe and the quay – with its variety of restaurants and cafés – is reminiscent of an Italian lakeside resort. Unfortunately, the small Venetian fort dating from 1212 is not open to the public, and all that is left of the former Turkish Quarter is a single, dilapidated mosque.

For the sake of the scenic drive and beautiful views back to the south coast, return to Aghios Nikólaos through the mountains via the towns of Anatolí, Kalamáfka and Prina (where you will find a welcome *tavérna* on the right-hand side as you enter town).

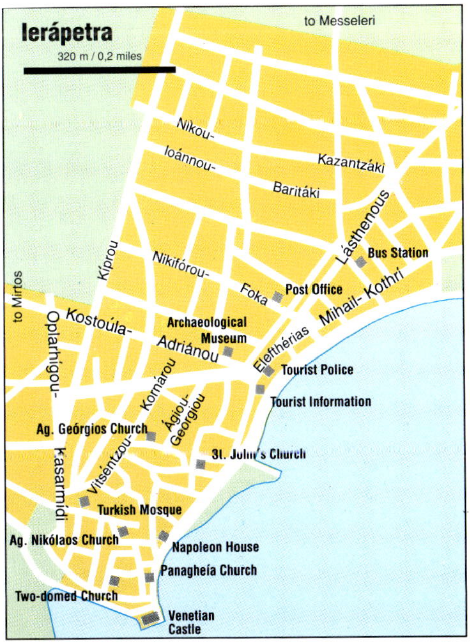

24. Eloúnda and Spinalónga

A popular resort; a scenic peninsula once used as a leper colony. A half-day's excursion. Take a bathing costume. See the map on page 80.

– Take the old Irákleion road and turn off right (signposted 9km/5 miles). –

For many years **Eloúnda** was the holiday resort frequented by so many Greek politicians. But like Aghios Nikólaos, it has undergone rapid development during recent years, due to its long sandy beach (which gets packed in summer), and has lost most of its glamour. The heights around Eloúnda contain mineral deposits unique in Greece. **Spinalónga Peninsula** curls around the bay creating the impression that Eloúnda lies beside an inland lake.

Below Eloúnda a road, suitable for vehicles, leads across to the peninsula. Stone windmills remain standing and you can still see the former saltworks, where the land was once settled, but the ancient city of **Oloús**, thought to have been the port of the Dorian city of Dréros, now lies below the waterline. When the sea is calm, you can still see the remains of Oloús's walls in the sea. Not much is known about this ancient city, but it was mentioned in documents of the 2nd century BC and in the writings of Pausanias, in the 2nd century AD. On the opposite side, to the right above a restaurant, have a look at the fenced-in mosaic floor of an Early Christian basilica.

In the summertime, boats leave hourly from Eloúnda for the island of **Spinalónga** – more properly, Kalydón – just off the peninsula's shore. In 1579, the Venetians turned the rock into a fort. With its 35 cannons, it was considered impregnable until the Turks finally managed to conquer it. During the uprisings against the Ottomans in the 19th century, many Turkish families fled into the

Eloúnda

Kalydón/Spinalónga: the former leper colony

stronghold, forming their own community of 1,112 people in 1834. They made their living through trade.

In 1903, the Cretan government established a leper colony here. Four hundred people suffering from Hansen's Disease who, until then, had been outcasts, now found a refuge. There were workshops, restaurants and shops on the islet; church services were held in two churches; plays were performed. The healthy children of afflicted parents were taken off Spinalónga.

It was not until 1957 that this last colony was closed. The residents were brought to a hospital, and the island was abandoned. As they fall into ruin, the buildings and the island cemetery tell their own poignant tale of courage and a visit here is inspirational.

Bringing this outing to a close, we recommend the short drive along the coast to the low-key resort of **Pláka**, with its arc-shaped pebble beach, award-winning crystal-clear waters and good selection of fish *tavérnes*. Enjoy the beautiful view of Spinalónga while tucking into your freshly fried squid or red mullet.

The old windmills north of Eloúnda

Eating

'Everything grown on Crete is infinitely better than the same things grown anywhere else.'

Plinius

Greek Cuisine

The common but erroneous assumption is that Greek cookery represents a deviant form of Turkish cuisine. In reality, Ottoman culinary arts benefited from rubbing shoulders with the independent, 2,500-year-old Greek tradition – which, on Crete, is even older.

The main ingredients bubbling in Cretan as well as in Greek pots are vegetables: peas and beans (since Minoan times, both fresh and dried); artichokes; wild greens; dandelions, leeks and spinach; various types of cabbage; wild asparagus; stalk celery and onions; as well as, since Columbus's voyage to America, potatoes, tomatoes, aubergines and corn. Leafy parsley, dill, mint, garlic, spring onions and, especially, lemons are all used as well in abundance.

Your table awaits

The main meal of the Cretan day is served at around 2pm, and consists of meat and vegetables or perhaps prawns; boiled leafy vegetables, dressed with olive oil and lemon juice; rice with spinach, or cooked blackeyed peas; fish, steamed in the oven with lemon wedges; tomatoes, bell peppers, grape leaves or zucchini (both fruit and blossoms) stuffed with rice, ground beef and herbs – the list of possibilities is a long one.

Stuffed grape and cabbage leaves, *stifádo* (spicy meat stew) and cheese puffs, as well as the popular sweets

Out

bougátsa and *loukoumáthes* were known to the Ancient Greeks.

The popularity of the omnipresent Greek salad, or *horiatikí saláta*, owes as much to the ease of preparation as to the seasonal availability of its obligatory ingredients, cucumbers and tomatoes. Otherwise, there is one salad available almost all year round: *maroúli*, like 'Romaine' lettuce, finely chopped and seasoned with olive oil, dill and spring onions. Also ubiquitous are salads made of white cabbage,

Tavérna tableware

spinach, carrots, small and large radishes and beetroot. The various vegetables may also be cooked and served as side dishes. Pork with *maroúli* or celery stalks, for example, is exquisite.

The staple tourist dish – grilled shish kebab, or *souvláki* – is rarely eaten in Cretan homes. Most restaurants serve 'fast *tavérna* food' – meat, or sometimes fish, on the grill; baked savoury puddings such as *pastítsio,* made with macaroni and minced meat; *moussaká*, made of potatoes and aubergines (often prepared in bulk in canteen kitchens) – all of which involve less work than the tastier, vegetable-intensive dishes.

The predominant Cretan attitude is that foreigners do not enjoy most traditional fare. Restaurant cuisine *per se* did not take hold in Greece, and thus also on Crete, until the advent of tourism in the 1960s – but now there are a few genuine gourmet restaurants, and you can take your pick of Indian, Chinese, Japanese, French or German cuisines in developed areas.

At the classic Greek *estiatórion*, the up-market cousin of the *tavérna*, you will find dishes also served in Greek homes, the preparation of which is an art form: chick pea or fish soup, broad beans with artichokes, stuffed vegetables or potatoes with chicken. The simpler version of the *estiatórion* is the *mayériko*, a cooking stall where you select your food directly from the hot stove. *Miá merítha* is one portion – ie, a plateful. It is not customary to take a bit of this and a bit of that from the various pots.

In *tavérnes*, the food is freshly prepared: that is, both fish and meat are prepared over the charcoal fire, either grilled or broiled; vegetables are deep-fried or steamed; various salads, among them *melitsanosaláta*, a sort of aubergine purée, and *taramosaláta*, a pureé of fish roe, are freshly made.

The classic among Cretan culinary venues is the *kafeneíon*. Here, at that bastion of the Greek male, the café, customers pass their time discussing politics, playing *távli* (Greek backgammon) and cards, reading newspapers or watching the passing parade. Here, they drink Greek coffee in small cups: *métrio*, medium sweet; *varí glikó*, strong and sweet; or *skéto*, without sugar. In recent years, instant coffee has become very popular – with 'Nescafé' standing in for all brands – hot with milk or cold in the form of a *frappé* with an ample head of foam. In the village *kafeneíon*, not off limits to women, the proprietor will also crack an egg into a skillet, make a salad or open a tin for hungry guests.

Except for the main dish, no food on a Greek table is private property. Everyone eats from all the plates and dishes, and empty glasses are always refilled. Normally, people also pay together, with the bill divided up equally and everyone chipping in.

Open-air fare

Cretan Venues

Tsigouthâthika or *rakáthika* are typical Cretan drinking venues where the traditional tipple of the island, the homemade white liquor, *tsigouthiá,* or *rakí*, similar to Italian *grappa*, is served, accompanied by various appetisers, *mezéthes*, which are quite filling. (One truly Cretan speciality is *oftés patátes*, potatoes roasted in their skins.) In an *ouzerí*, on the other hand, *oúzo* is the main drink. Many street corners have *souvlatzíthika*, where you eat chunks of grilled meat with bites of tomato, chopped onions and *tzatzíki* (yoghourt, cucumber, garlic and dill) – all wrapped up in pitta bread, either on the spot or as a takeaway.

Desserts

The *zakaroplasteíon* specialises in all kinds of sweets: from ice-cream to *rizógalo* (rice pudding), puddings, pies and cake-like pastries, such as *bougátsa, loukoumáthes* and *pástes*. Fresh oranges and man-

Traditional cheeses

darins for dessert have only been popular since around 1500, and coffee, which today seems so essential to the Greek way of life, arrived in Greece and Crete from Ethiopia in around 1600.

Celebrations and Nightlife

The *kritiká kéntra*, traditional nightclubs located on the edges of towns or even further out in the country, are important addresses for weddings, or evenings of live Cretan music. People also come here to eat and drink, but mainly to dance Cretan dances. The *skiláthika* are similar but sleazier clubs – actually imports from the mainland – their dance music furnished by second- or third-rate *bouzoúki* ensembles. Whisky is sold by the bottle for steep prices. A *skiláthiko* is the final stop of many a late-evening tour of the nightspots. In addition, there are plenty of discos, and countless café-bars where you can order anything from coffee to whisky.

The restaurants, cafés and bars listed below are predominately patronised by locals and are not always easy to find, so you will need a taxi. These places will give you a good idea of everyday cooking and dining out on Crete. So: *Kalí órexi* – enjoy your meal!

'Wedding rings'

Dining in Chaniá

Restaurants proliferate around the Venetian harbour and city walls. Though large sections of their menus are fairly touristy, you will find plenty of authentic Cretan cuisine too.

AERIKO, *taverna/ouzerí;* Aktí Miaoúli in the quarter of Kum Kapí.

TAMAM, *estiatórion;* in a former Turkish bath at Odós Zambelíou 49, on the harbour.

GONIA, a tiny restaurant with western Cretan specialities such as *sfakianés pítes* and *kalitsoúnia*, cheese puffs from Sfakiá and Chaniá. Opens at 6pm. Odós Polichronídi 33/corner of Odós Geróla in the quarter of Páno Kum Kapí.

LES VAGABONDS, restaurant and jazz club; Odós Pórtou 44.

ADIÉKSODO,an *ouzeri* offering live Greek music in the evenings. Theotokópoulou 59.

BINGASA, *estiatórion.* To the west of town in Galatás on the main road. Turkish and Greek food.

KULURIDIS, *tavérna* in Vamvakópoulo. Follow the signs southwest along the road to Alikianós. Very good cuisine, but not cheap.

MALAXA, a small *tavérna* in the village of the same name to the east of town. The house speciality is *stáka*, a tasty porridge of cream and flour, eaten with bread.

KIANI AKTI, classical fish *tavérna* under tamarisks directly by the sea on the road to the east just this side of Kalíves (closed in winter).

MELTEMAKIA, fish *tavérna* by the seafront on the road from Soúda in the direction of the airport, in Wlités at the end of the bay (closed from December through to February).

BARBAS LEFTÉRIS, *tavérna* in Kamissianá, just this side of Kolimbári towards the west of town.

FAKA (The Mousetrap), in the shadows of the Venetian arsenal. Outside dining. Eschew the tourist dishes such as moussaka and go for a mezze.

ÁNEMOS, restaurant right at the heart of things on Aktí Tombázi.

FAGOTTO, bar, Odós Angélon 16. In an old vaulted building near the Firkás Fortress.

EN PLO, a quiet *tavérna* located at Pórtou 13.

MELTÉMI, *kafeneíon* next to the Marine Museum.

CLUB ARIADNI, disco, Aktí Tombási next to the Central Port Authority.

STREET, disco bar, the old harbour.

TA DYO LOUX, Odós Sarpidóna. Coffee place for local trendies where you can practise your *tavli*.

Dining in Réthymnon

'isitors are spoilt for choice in ₹éthymnon. Remember, restaurants on he harbour are often far more expensive than those in the back streets.

AVLI, restaurant; Odós Xanthoudídou, orner of Odós Radámanthos. Very efined, with candlelight and soothing piano music.

KIRIA MARIA, *mayériko* on Odós Moschowíti close to the Rimondi Fountain.

SOKAKI, *tavérna/estiatórion* ; Odós Pórtou 6 (closed in the winter).

BALUARDI, *mezethopolíon* (equivalent to a *tsigouthátiko*); on the shore drive below the Fortézza near the harbour.

TO METHISMENO FEGGARI, ('The Drunken Moon'), *ouzerí/kafeneíon*, Odós Melisínou 34.

JEORJIOS, *rakáthiko*, below the Archaeological Museum (closed in the winter months).

BABIS, *rakáthiko*; Odós Ag. Barbáras 13. Here they serve only traditional dishes of *oftés patátes*, green olives and *tsigouthiá/rakí*.

KOMBOS, *tavérna* in Violí Haráki on the old road to Chaniá.

MILTOS, in Maroulás, to the west of town. A *tavérna* serving two hot dishes a day, such as lentils or aubergines.

TO ELLINIKON, a *mezedopoleíon* situated near the Rimondi Fountain.

HELONA (The Turtle), a fish *tavérna* on the Venetian Harbour.

VENETSIANIKO, a café-bar on the Venetian Harbour.

ANGELA'S, Odós Dikastírion. The best place for squid.

O PSARAS, simple, typical fish *tavérna*. Odós Arambatsóglu 69 (formerly Odós Thessaloníkis). Try *stifádo* with *ochtapódi* (octopus in red sauce).

SESILIA, bar, Prokiméa E Venizélou.

VASILIKO, popular café-bar at the Rimondi Fountain.

TAVERNA MINARÉS, a Greek *tavérna* by the Nerantzés Mosque.

FORTETZA, a disco located on the Venetian harbour.

Dining in Irákleion

IONIA, *mayériko* on Chatzimiháli Giánnari. Good hearty Greek food.

PLATANOS (The plane tree), *ouzeri* and coffee shop under the plane tree in Pl. Ághios Títos. Beautiful place for a relaxing snack or drink right in the centre of town.

3/4, restaurant, bar-café; Odós Theotokopoúlou 1. In a pretty, neoclassical building on the old harbour; very refined.

GIOVANNI, sophisticated *tavérna*, Odós Koraí.

Shouldering the empties

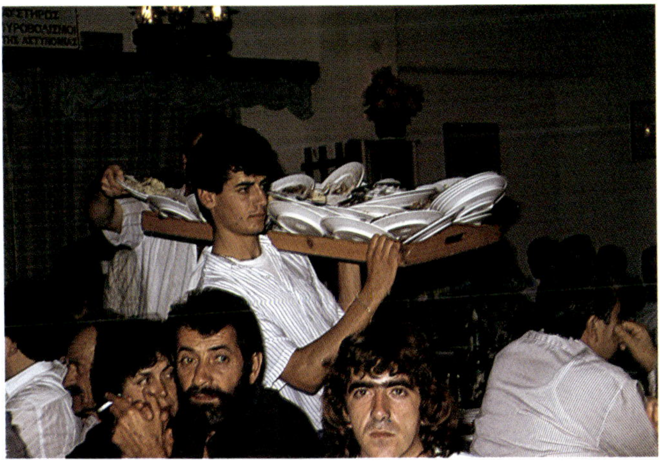

Ippokambos ('Sea Horse'), *ouzerí*; Odós Mitsotáki 3, on the old harbour (closed from 3.30-7pm).

Malandris, *mayériko* hidden off the fish market on Odós Bizaníou. Local venue for the market workers; open all times; especially good for lunch.

Vardia (Shift), *ouzerí* on the old harbour, opens at 4pm.

Konstandin Lidakis, café–bar in Arhánes, opposite the Panagheía Church with its three naves on the main road.

Kirkor, a tiny shop at the Morosoni Fountain; sells puff-pastry sweetmeats with a cream cheese or sweet cream filling – also available to take out.

Rakadika, on Odós Pediádos and Odós Víglas. Serves traditional Cretan *rakádika*.

Tromboni, 'boite' with live gigs, Odós S Venizélou, corner of Melidóni.

Flu, Plateía Daskalogiánni. (*Flu* means 'out of focus'.)

Notos, **Milon tis Eridos** and **Avgo**, bars at the end of Odós Koraí.

Onar, café and tea-room; Odos Chandakos 36B.

Drawing in the punters

Dining in Aghios Nikólaos

Bland English/international food much in evidence thanks to the larg number of English tourists who com to Aghios Nikólaos. To avoid suc food, try the following:

Tavern Aouas, *tavérna* with tables an garden, Odós Paleológou, 100r (110yds) from the Folklore Museum Numerous hot dishes.

Tavern the Pine, traditional *estiatórion* by the lake, Paleologou 18 by a palm tree.

Faros, fish *tavérna* with seaside view on Kitroplateía Beach.

La Casa, café/restaurant, Odós 28 Oktombríou, with lake view.

Aktéon, a simple *tavérna* along th harbour.

The Café, above the lake on Odós N Plastira. Café-bar with great views.

To Pélagos, fish tavérna in a beautifu building on the corner of Odós Str Kóraka and Odós Kapetán Fafoúti Also traditional Cretan food.

Sarris, Greek food and grill.

O Sigos, *estiatórion* in Kaló Horió or the road to Sitía.

Café Plaza, next to the Folklore Museum. Rather chic and expensive for some tastes, but right in the heart of things.

Bora-Bora, **Lipstick**, **Studio**, **Yianni's Bar**, **Mithos Club**, and **Nine Muses**: all very popular discotheques along the harbour.

Fish *Tavérnes* in Pláka

Fifteen kilometres (9 miles) north of Aghios Nikólaos and with a view of Spinalónga Island is Pláka, ideal for lunch or dinner and much quieter than its neighbour Eloúnda. Among the fish tavernas try **Manolis** or **Gorgona** on the seafront.

Shopping

Ceramics, embroidery work, hand woven fabrics, knits and metal and wood crafts, as well as spices and herbal teas – such as mint, sage and *díktamo* – are all popular souvenirs that have been important export commodities on Crete as far back as

A street cluttered with souvenirs

Minoan times. The shops are concentrated in the town centre areas of Chaniá, Réthymnon (which offers the best shopping on the island), Irákleion and Aghios Nikólaos. Souvenirs shops, selling plenty of kitsch and junk, are easy to recognise – and avoid.

What to buy

Spices

In Chaniá, for example, the covered market is truly a paradise for spice fans: from curry to red peppercorns to Cretan saffron in three different strengths, you can find everything here. Choose from spicy cinammon bark, boiled to make tea in the winter, along with the most important spice in Greek cooking, next to the lemon, *rígani*, or wild marjoram.

Household Goods

Small household goods shops and market vendors sell sturdy, woven wicker baskets, as well as light airy ones out of bamboo, wonderful wooden spoons and the traditional *bríki* – the small copper coffee pot with the long handle. With a bit of luck, you can also find the matching long-handled copper spoon and the whisk, the Greek coffee implements which have been out of fashion for quite some time. You may have to look for a chinaware store to get the tiny cups to go with the set: the classical *kafeneíon* variety are white and unbreakable. To round out your coffee utensils you also need a brass coffee grinder. The smaller versions of these mills double quite well as peppergrinders.

Cretan Knives

Long and curved, in silver scabbards and with thick white handles, these weapons were originally part of the traditional costume. The old ones are rare and expensive, but they also come in various shapes and sizes as souvenirs. However, there is also a whole range of other knives, from chopping knives to the curved knives used to prune the grape vines (or *ambélia*).

Fabrics

Hand woven top-quality fabrics and blankets, usually on a red background, are still, like hand-embroidered or crocheted blankets, important products of the native crafts industry, although industrial copies are stepping up competition. Inexpensive items are sheep's wool knits and countless cotton products from T-shirts to towels, as well as conventional linens with colourful or monochrome stripes on a white background. These get softer with every washing.

Leather Goods

Crete is famous for its leathergoods: bags in all sizes, rucksacks, sandals and especially boots of cowhide imported from Africa.

Ceramics/Earthenware

Unglazed storage jars of the kind produced on Crete 4,000 years ago and usually used as flower pots today, plus other pots and jugs of all sizes are often sold along the roads just outside towns. There is also a great deal of everyday earthenware, some of it quite pretty.

Jewellery

Gold and silver are relatively inexpensive in Greece, which explains the abundance of jewellery shops – often selling machine-made merchandise. Still, there are a number of skilled gold- and silversmiths.

Printed Matter

If you are interested in additional information about Crete, you can pick up literature and maps at the international bookshops, as well as at kiosks.

Music

We recommend you sample some of the records or cassettes by the best known and loved Cretan musicians, such as Psarantónis and his band from Anóghia, who do interpretations – often quite unconventional ones, at that – of traditional, folk music. His *Erotókritos*, Crete's 'national' 17th-century epic, is wonderful. For something completely different, on a soft lyrical note, try the love songs and laments (*erotiká* and *mirolóya*), which Ludovíkos of Anóghia collected among the women of his village. The recordings by Ross Daly, as well, an Irishman who has practically become a Cretan, are especially creative, his *Lavírinthos*, for example. This is also true of the albums by the famous and beloved singer who died at an early age, Níkos Xilúris, Psarantónis's brother. The music by a *lyra* player who 'emigrated' to Piraeus, Kóstas Mountákis, is to be highly recommended as well.

Gold is relatively cheap

Culinary Products

Returning to the subject of food and drink, there are a number of products worth taking back home with you, including the sharp, firm cheese, *graviéra*; honey (*méli*), especially the kind derived from thyme blossoms; wine from the Kastélli Kissamós to Sitía; and *tsigouthiá*, Crete's version of *oúzo*.

You can also stock up on *pássa témpo* from any of the numerous street carts: these are paper bags full of peanuts in salted shells, pistachios, roasted chick peas and pumpkin seeds, all for the journey home.

Street in Réthymnon

Shopping in Chaniá

The **covered market** on Plateía S Venizélou offers a wide selection of all Crete's various herbs, spices, cheeses and honeys. Odós Skrídlof, the extension of Odós Tsouderón below the market, leading to Odós Chálidon, is the street of the *stivanáthika*, the **bootmakers-cum-leathergoods-retailers**, where you can also buy bags and sandals, rucksacks and belts. During the summer months, the street is so crowded that pedestrians can hardly get through. The surrounding lanes are the place to watch one of these bootmakers at work. The leather products are good, durable and fairly reasonably priced.

For everyday pottery such as ashtrays, vases and cups, try the **Trochós Ceramics Workshop** next to the Archaeological Museum on the same street. Beautiful, authentic pottery can also be found at **Handmade Cretan Ceramics**, Odós Zambelíou 81.

The international **bookshop**, hidden behind all the postcard stands, stocks a wide range of foreign language books on Crete. Not far from Aktí Tombási, the Artisan's Cooperative of Chaniá runs a show- and sales-room with exhibits of **hand-woven goods** such as table-cloths, blankets and carpets, as well as **ceramics**. For colourful **rugs and carpets** made on the premises, go to **Róka**, Zambelíou 61. For **woven handicrafts**, try **Yfandá**, Odós Isodíon 19.

Those with a penchant for the genuine article in **spirits** should go to the General Store at Odós Grigoríou 16 (one block up from the city hall, *dimarhío*, opposite the Fire Station). Here you can still buy wine (*krassí*), brandy (*konyák*) and *tsigouthiá*, all right out of the barrel. Below the covered market on Odós Potié, there is a small shop specialising in távli, the Greek version of backgammon, as well as chess sets. And the famous *maherádika*, the traditional **Cretan knives shops** all along Odós Sífaka are also worth a visit.

Shopping in Réthymnon

The main shopping streets in Réthymnon are: Odós Arkadíou, Odós Iróön Politechníou, Odós Paleológou and Odós Gerkári. Here you'll find Crete's **culinary delights** galore: honey and herbs, pickled or black and green olives in brine, spices and cheese – plus the richly ornamented wedding cakes, more a decoration today than a delicacy. On Odós Paleológou, diagonally opposite the Venetian loggia, there is an **off-licence** which even sells self-bottled *tsigouthiá* or *rakí*. You should at least have a look at the **Faskómilo** (sage) **Herb Shop** on Odós Soulíou, a truly original, witty store where each little packet of herbs is labelled with often unconventional suggested usage. The tiny leaves and branches of the *sarantothéndri* (the 'forty tree') are good for ailments of the duodenum, the gall bladder and the liver; and, as a seasoning for shish kebab and pizza, the house recommends thyme '... without wood, without dirt, without dust...'

The international **bookshop** at the corner of Odós I Peticháki and Prokiméa E Venizélou stocks a good selection, including translations of Greek literature, art and nature guide books about Crete and excursions from Crete, as well as **prints** of old views of the city and maps of the island. In the Venetian Loggia is the **Archaeological Museum Shop**, which specialises in copies of museum exhibits plus books and videos related to the museum.

Shopping in Irákleion

Odós 1866 is to Irákleion what the covered market is to Chaniá: a colourful, bustling bazaar with countless stands selling all the culinary delights Crete has to offer. Also hidden in this street you have one of those simple old Greek hotels with rooms containing up to four beds. One of the small sidestreets features one hot food stall and *tavérna* after another. After a night of drinking, people come here at dawn to eat *patsás*, a soup made of tripe, purportedly to clear their heads. The major shopping streets are Odós Kalokerinóu, leading to the Pórta Chanión in the west, Odós 25 Avgoústou, Odós Dikeosínis, Odós Dedálou and its parallel street, Odós Koraï.

City kiosk

Irákleion is full of antique shops – although not everything which is sold as such is actually antique – and buyers must beware of paying top money for copies. But a pretty copy can be very pleasing at a good price. You will find many books on Irákleion and Crete at the international **bookshop** on Odós 25 Avgoústou. For travel books, try **Planet** at the corner of Chándaka and Kidonías. The most beautiful bookshop on the island is **Naftilos** on Odós Koraï – one of the prettiest little streets in town. Browsing may make you wish you could read Greek, but you can at least buy a print of a Merian engraving of Irákleion.

Opposite the Archaeological Museum on Plateía Eleftherías, Eléni Kastrinoyánni's shop is well known for **handwoven fabrics**. If it is **jewellery** you have in mind, some of it patterned upon Byzantine prototypes, you will find it at Fanourákis on Plateía Fokás. Fanourakis, a Cretan jeweller, has shops in Athens as well, and his designs are especially well liked by Athenians who find Zolotas and Lalaounis too mass produced.

Shopping in Aghios Nikólaos

In this youngest and smallest of the island's urban centres, shopping is limited to the two streets beginning at the harbour, Odós Koundoúrou and Odós 28 Oktomvríou. Here, too, you have the ubiquitous jewellery and leathergoods shops.

The **arts and crafts shop** on Odós 28 Oktomvríou is steeped in tradition. Many years ago, owner Sofía Kaná gave up journalism for weaving. She collects all the plants she uses to make dyes for her **carpets**, and many women have since learned old dyeing methods from her. Also worth a mention is a little shop a few doors up the street, which sells cotton, woollen and wool/silk knitwear. Like many others, it is closed from November to April, so if you miss it try the **knitting factory**, *to plektírio*, on Odós Ethnikís Antístasis or the **designer T-shirt** shop, **Zoe's**, at Paleológou 1.

Replicas abound

Calendar of Special Events

Saints' Days

The *paniyíria* are among the most important dates on the Cretan calendar of celebrations. These festive events honouring the patron saints of monasteries always begin the day before. In the old days, people converged on the monastery, either on foot, or by mule or donkey, bags and baskets packed with blankets for the night, wicker-covered flasks of wine and parcels of food.

The 'name days' of the churches' saints are equally important and particularly beautiful at small, remote churches. This is also one reason why there is at least a gravel road leading to even the most remote and tiny church. In the churches, priests pass out *ártos*, consecrated, sweet, white bread, sometimes followed by wine, salted fish and ordinary bread. Since there are many monasteries and churches, there is an enormous number of saints' days celebrated.

Here is a selection of these religious celebrations, along with the other festive and memorial days:

1st Sunday after Easter *Aghios Thomás* at the Vrondíssi Monastery/Irákleion.

23 April *Aghios Geórgios* in many villages, if Easter is late – otherwise on Easter Monday.

8 May *O Ioánnis o Theológos* (John the Evangelist) Préveli Monastery/Réthymnon.

20–27 May *Ee Máchi tis Krítis* (The Battle of Crete), commemoration of the German air attack in 1941.

25 May Celebrations are held in Hóra Sfakión commemorating the 1821 Revolution.

24 June *Ioánnis o Próthromos* (John the Baptist) and midsummer celebrations.

20 July *Profítis Ilías* (Prophet Elijah), on mountain peaks and in many villages.

Priests preside

Singing celebrants on the day the new wine is tasted

26 July	*Aghios Paraskeví*, popular celebration at the Skotinó Grotto in Nomós Irákleion, district of Pediáda.
July	Wine festival in Réthymnon.
6 August	*Metamórfosis*, the Transfiguration of Christ, on Mount Yoúchtas near Arhánes.
15 August	*Ed Kímissis tis Panagheías*, Assumption of the Virgin Mary, at the monasteries of Chrissoskalítissa, Faneroménis etc.
25 August	*Aghios Títos* in Irákleion.
27 August	*Aghios Fanúorios* at Valsamónero Monastery.
14 September	*Tímios Stavrós*, the Raising of the Cross in Axós and Anóghia, Réthymnon; procession to Aféndis Stavroménos.
3 November	*Aghios Geórgios o Methistís*, Saint George, who 'makes the others drunk' – this is the day when the new wine and the fresh *tsigouthiá* are tasted.
7–9 November	National holiday at the Arkádi Monastery.
11 November	*Aghios Minás*, patron saint of Irákleion.
21 November	*Panagheías Isodia*, Mary's introduction to the Temple, the patron saint of Chanía and Réthymnon.
3 December	*Aghios Nikólaos*, patron saint of the city.

On the home front

Practical Information

TRAVEL ESSENTIALS

When to Visit

Crete is always enjoyable, even if there are some low-hanging clouds in November, or a little thunder, or even several hours of the rain that is so anxiously awaited by the olive growers. Visitors who are interested only in lying on the beach will choose to come in midsummer, despite the overcrowding and the heat. But, for getting to know the island well, the spring and autumn are much better seasons, with ideal weather for hikes and outings.

Winter, in fact, is the perfect time to come if you are particularly interested in studying the Palace of Knossós and the Archaeological Museum in Irákleion, with its numerous Minoan holdings. In winter you can wander unhurried and unhampered by masses of other visitors. Along the coast, temperatures never fall below freezing, whereas the mountains may be covered in snow until spring.

Visa Requirements

For a stay of up to three months, travellers from EU states, the United States or Canada do not need a visa; a passport or identification card is required. Anyone intending to stay for a longer period must apply for a residence permit.

Arriving by Air

Most visitors to Crete arrive by air these days, on direct charter or regularly scheduled flights. From November to March, however, you must change planes in Athens. Airports of arrival are Chaniá and Irákleion – and still, occasionally, Sitía.

Arriving by Sea

The classic way to reach the island is by sea. The ferries, all belonging to Cretan shipping lines (ANEK, Minoan Lines and Rethimniakí Lines), ply the waters between Chaniá's port, Soúda, Irákleion and Réthymnon and Piraeus daily. The ships are large and comfortable, the food is inexpensive and there are cabins available, for the crossings usually take place at night.

During the summer months, there are frequent ship connections with Santoríni; once a week (all year around) a ship sails from Piraeus via the Cycladic Islands, and from Crete to Rhodes and back; as well as from Kastélli/Kíssamos via Kythira to the Peloponnese. For yachts, the ports of call are Chaniá and Irákleion.

Electricity

In Greece, the electricity is 220 volts. You can get adaptors for the various electrical sockets from any supermarket.

Clothing

In summer, bring light clothing made of natural fabrics; we recommend a wind-breaker, jersey and sturdy shoes for evenings on board ship, at the seaside or on hikes. From December to March, you do not need a heavy coat, but you should pack ample pullovers and a rain coat, since it is often damp and both apartments and public places are often poorly heated. Sometimes, it is warmer outside than inside.

TOURIST INFORMATION

We recommend you visit an EOT (Greek Tourist Organisation) information office or the local authorities (Tourist Police), where information and hotel lists are freely available.

Chaniá (EOT) Pántheon Building, Odós Kriári 40. Tel (0821) 92943, 92624, 7am–3pm.

Réthymnon (EOT) Prokiméa E. Venizélou. Tel (0831) 29148, 9am–2.30pm.

Irákleion (EOT) Odós Xanthoudídou 1, opposite the Archaeological Museum. Tel (081) 228203, 8.30am–2.30pm.

Aghios Nikólaos (Municipal Tourist Information Office) Aktí I Koúndourou 20. Tel (0841) 22357, 8.30am–9.30pm in the tourist season only.

Import unlimited foreign currency

MONEY MATTERS

You can change money at airports and frontier crossings, in hotels, bureaux de change and banks, but post offices offer the best rates. There are ATMs outside the main banks in city centres.

The Greek currency is the drachma. There are notes from 100 to 10,000 drachmas and coins from five to 100 drachmas. It is prohibited to import more than 100,000 drachmas, but you can import any amount of foreign currency. In theory, you should declare amounts over £250/US$500 upon entering if you think you may want to take this money back out of the country when you leave. Strikes permitting, banks are open Monday to Friday, 8.30am–2pm.

ACCOMMODATION

In the busy months of July and August it is best to reserve rooms in advance as many hotels are fully booked. An alternative to hotel accommodation is the economical and much used rooms-for-rent system, which usually involves sharing a bathroom with other tenants, often in the proprietor's own house. It is acceptable to inspect these rooms before renting them.

Rooms for rent can be found by wandering around the town looking for the signs. Prices vary according to the season, though discounts are usually made for stays of more than three days. The Greek tourist organization EOT can generally point you in their direction – call EOT in advance to check availability at your destination.

Aghios Nikólaos

ELOUNDA BAY (deluxe)
Eleven km (7 miles) north of Aghios Nikólaos in Eloúnda
Tel (0841) 41580
Rooms and bungalows, restaurant, beach and pool. Open April to October.

Ermis (category A)
Akti I, Koúndouro
Tel (0841) 28253
Restaurant, pool, 389 beds. Open from April to October.

Coral (category B)
Akti I, Koúndouro
Tel (0841) 28363
Restaurant, pool, 323 beds. Open from April to October.

El Greco (Category B)
Kitroplateía Beach
Tel (0841) 28894
Restaurant, parking, 87 beds. Open from March to October.

Sgouros (category C)
Akti Pangálou, Kitroplateía Beach
Tel (0841) 28931
Restaurant, parking, 52 beds, on the beach. Open from March to October.

Ákratos (category C)
28 Oktovríou, on the lake
Tel (0841) 22721
Restaurant, parking, 59 beds, 300 metres (330 yards) from the sea. Open from April to October.

Du Lac (category C)
28 Oktovríou no. 27, on the lake
Tel (0841) 22711
Parking, 60 beds, 500 metres (550 yards) from the sea. Open from April to October.

Chania

Amphora (category A)
Theotokópoulou
Tel (0821) 93224
Traditional style, restaurant, 42 beds, 500 metres (550 yards) from the sea.

Kidon (category A)
Pl. S. Venizélou
Tel (0821) 52280
Access for disabled people, restaurant, 191 beds, TV, parking. Open all year.

Casa Delfino (category B)
Theophanoús 9, off Theotokópoulou
Tel (0821) 93098
Traditional style, 31 beds, air conditioning, bar, TV. Open all year.

Xenia (category B)
On the seafront by Fort Fírkas
Tel (0821) 91238
Restaurant, 88 beds, pool, parking. Open all year.

Doma (category B)
El. Venizélou 124
Tel (0821) 51772
Traditional style, restaurant, 48 beds, 10 metres (11 yards) from the sea, parking. Open March to October.

Nostos (category B)
Zambelíou 42–46
Tel (0821) 94740
Traditiona, 27 beds, 200 metres (220 yards) from the sea. Open April to October.

ELLINIS (category C)
Tzanakáki 68
Tel (0821) 58070
Parking, 59 beds. Open all year.

Irákleion

XENIA (category A)
S. Venizélou 2
Tel (081) 284000/1
Parking, 156 beds, restaurant, on the seafront. Open April to December.

KAPSIS BEACH (category A)
Agía Pelagía, 20km (13 miles) west of Irákleion
Tel (081) 811112
Restaurant, 1,300 beds, pool and beach. Open March to November.

GALAXY (category A)
Dimokratías 67
Tel (081) 238812
Pool, 264 beds, restaurant, air conditioning. Open all year.

LATO (category B)
Epimenídou 15
Tel (081) 228103
Ninety-nine beds. Open all year.

ÁTRION (category B)
Paleológou 9
Tel (081) 229225
Parking, 117 beds, air-conditioning, TV. Open all year.

KASTRO (category B)
Theotokópoulou 22
Tel (081) 285020
Parking, 63 beds. Open all year.

KRIS (category C)
Bofór 2
Tel (081) 223211
Parking, 17 beds, pool. Open all year.

MARIN (category C)
Bofór 10
Tel (081) 220737
Parking, 83 beds. Open all year.

Réthymnon

RÉTHIMNA BEACH (deluxe)
Ádele Beach, 8km (5 miles) northeast of Réthymnon
Tel (0831) 71002
Rooms and bungalows, 1,042 beds, air-conditioning, TV. Open from April to November.

PORTO RÉTHIMNO (category A)
S. Venizélou 52A
Tel (0831) 51980
Restaurant, 400 beds, pool, 25 metres (27 yards) from the sea. Open from April to November.

KYMA BEACH (category B)
Giaboudáki 2, close to town centre
Tel (0831) 55503
Restaurant, 64 beds, seasports, TV, air conditioning. Open all year.

FORTÉZZA (category B)
Melissinoú 16
Tel (0831) 55551
Restaurant, 102 beds, swimming pool and parking. Open from March to November.

Skaléta Beach (category B)
Skaléta, 15km (9 miles) outside of Réthymnon
Tel (0831) 71702
Restaurant, 216 beds, pool. Open from April to October.

Ádele Beach Bungalows (category B)
Ádele Beach, 8km (5 miles) north-east of Réthymnon
Tel (0831) 71047
Restaurant, 150 beds, pool. Open from March to November.

Brascos (category B)
Daskaláki 1
Tel (0831) 23721
Restaurant, 156 beds, parking. Open from March to October.

Idaion (category B)
Pl. N. Plastíra 10
Tel (0831) 28667
Restaurant, 160 beds, 50 metres (55 yards) from the sea, parking. Open from March to October.

GETTING ACQUAINTED

Geography and Topography

Crete is 260km (162 miles) long, 12–60km (7–37 miles) wide, and the coastline is 1,046km (650 miles) in length. It is the largest of the Greek islands and the fifth largest in the Mediterranean. The most characteristic feature of the landscape is the silvery olive trees, whose cultivation was intensified during the rule of the Turks.

The geography of Crete is largely determined by three high massifs: the Lefka Ori (White Mountains) to the west with its highest peak, the Páchnes (2,452m/8,045ft); the Ida range, or Psiloritis (2,456m/8,058ft) in the centre; and the Díkti Mountains in the east (2,148m/7,047ft). The mountains in the east are gentler, with the highest peak, the Aféndis Stavroménos, reaching 1,476m/4,843ft. Crete owes its over 3,000 caves – approximately half of all the caves in Greece – and its numerous ravines to the crystalline consistency of its limestone crust. The majority of Crete's underground cavities have yet to be explored.

The gorges are predominantly located on the southern half of the island, the longest and most famous being the Samariá Gorge. There are two large

Interior landscape

and several smaller fertile plateaux, as well as two large bays along the northern coast.

The last census recorded Crete's population at 520,000. More than half of this number live in the Nomós Irákleion. Crete is divided into four *nomí*, governmental regions: Chaniá, Réthymnon and Irákleion, with their respective regional capitals of the same names; and Lassíthi, with Aghios Nikólaos as its capital. The individual *nomí* are then subdivided into districts, or *eparchíes*. In 1972, Irákleion replaced Chaniá as the capital of the entire island. On Crete there are 11 cities and 1,447 villages.

Weather

Hippocrates, the great doctor of antiquity, recommended that anyone convalescing from a severe illness should seek out the mild climate of Crete. With an average of 320 sunny days per year, the average temperature in the summer is 30–35°C (86–95°F), rarely rising as high as 40°C (104°F); in the winter it is 10–18°C (50–65°F); and while the water never gets above about 25°C (about 77°F) in the summer, it is a fairly warm 15–21°C (60–70°F) during the winter months.

The hottest month of the year is July, when conditions can become African in the truest sense of the word. Then, in addition to the hot sun, the scorching desert wind, the *livas,* blows in from the south. But from whichever direction the winds blow, they are a decisive factor. When the wind speed rises above eight on the Beaufort Scale, which happens quite frequently, especially in the exposed far eastern side of the island, nothing can leave port, not even the very largest ferries.

During the period between the end of May and the last week of August, a northerly trade wind prevails, the *meltémi*, blowing for about 15 days at a time. The Turkish Cretans coined poetic epithets, such as 'grape *meltémi*', for this wind.

In the summer months, you should always take the sun seriously. Avoid going out during the hottest hours at midday, using sun protection at all times and wearing a sun hat. If you do overheat, avoid ice-cold drinks, which may exacerbate problems.

Holiday illness is frequently a result of too much sun, especially when combined with a heavy intake of alcohol.

Flora and Fauna

The vast wooded areas of prehistoric Crete are no more: deforestation and grazing have left but two percent of the land area covered with trees. These are mainly cypresses, pines, oaks, chestnuts, planes, pines, tamarisks, juniper and eucalyptus trees. There are over 2,000 botanical species on Crete, of which a tenth are indigenous. They include numerous herbs, the most sought after being the *díkatamos*, a wonder drug effective in curing all sorts of illnesses and very tasty.

In addition to the native wild goat, the *krí-krí* – today a protected species – there are hares, rabbits, martens, small eagles, hawks, buzzards, lamb vultures and numerous butterflies on Crete. There are no poisonous snakes on the island. The camel's stint as a pack animal here ended with the Turkish withdrawal from the island, and the job was left to the mules and donkeys. As throughout the rest of the Mediterranean, the fish population in Crete's seas has gone down sharply.

Agriculture

Despite the growth of tourism, Crete still has an agricultural economy, although only about 35 percent of the land can be cultivated. The most important crops are olives, sultanas, table grapes, tomatoes, cucumbers, citrus fruits, wine, bananas and carob. Crete's flocks of sheep and goats do produce some meat but primarily wool and various types of cheese.

Earthquakes

The major portion of Crete belongs to Greece's earthquake-prone southern arc. The island lies on the Aegean Fault, which is no deeper than 500–800m (1,640–2,625ft), and there is a rift running through the southern part of the island, reaching a depth of 5,000m (3 miles). The last earthquake on Crete was in 1959.

GETTING AROUND

Taxis

Taxis and radio taxis are affordable and readily available; they can also be flagged down on the street. By taking taxis you benefit from the driver's knowledge of the area. Prices are fixed and should be agreed before you set off – especially for airport trips.

Buses

The municipal and rural bus systems (KTEL) are reliable, punctual and cheap. Each city has its own bus terminal (marked on the city maps) – ask for the 'KTEL'. Timetables in English can be obtained there, as well as in travel agencies, tourist information bureaux and at the airport when you arrive.

Car and Motorcycle Rentals

The number of car and motorcycle rental shops are legion; in fact, of late, you can even rent bicycles. We recommend you first look over both the vehicle and the insurance conditions very carefully. Many of the travel agencies also rent vehicles.

If you rent a vehicle in advance of arriving in Crete, through an international company, beware of hefty late-night collection charges. Generally it is cheaper to hire locally.

Petrol Stations

Petrol stations are open on weekdays from 7am–7pm; Saturday until 3pm. Certain petrol stations are also open all night and on Sunday. Unleaded petrol is available at all stations.

Road Safety

There is a good network of roads, and what your road map may still show as a gravel road, may be already paved. A word of caution, nevertheless. The Cretan style of driving, being more on the defensive side, takes some getting used to. High speeds – usually not possible anyway – are not recommended, if you want to avoid hair-raising surprises, whether it be that unexpected vehicle pulling into the road, a huge pothole or rock, or an entire herd of sheep suddenly looming up around the bend. Although usually ignored, the use of seatbelts in cars is required by law, as are helmets for motorcyclists.

Sturdy transport is best

The maximum speeds permitted on the national highway are: 100km/h (62mph) for cars, 70km/h (43mph) for other vehicles; the speed limit on country roads is 70km/h (43mph) and within towns usually 50km/h (31mph). On highways, motorists frequently use the hard shoulder as an extra lane, but visitors are advised not to.

If you get a parking or speeding fine, take the ticket to a police station or pay the car rental firm and be sure to get a receipt.

Maps and Guide Books

There are many street and road maps and guide books on the market with details of cities, museums, excavation sites, flora and fauna. So fact fiends can build up a small library simply by stopping off at the nearest central kiosk, or *períptero*, or any of the foreign-language bookshops. The maps are not always accurate.

Hiking

The few services to hikers on Crete are provided through the Greek Alpinists' Club. The number of viable trails is dwindling, as more and more of the old footpaths are turned into graded roads. However, in collaboration with the Alpinists' Club, the few tour promoters offering hiking holidays have started to mark some of the trails with coloured dots.

Excursions

Recommended gear: a pocket torch (flashlight), sturdy shoes and, even in summer, a jacket or sweater. For remote

Taking a well-earned break

areas, a foot pump as well as a spare tyre is a good idea. A thermos jug of water and an early start are absolute musts in summer. Around 2–6pm is siesta time everywhere, including any of the monasteries you may want to visit. In the villages, the *kafeneíon* is the local 'information office' for overnight accommodation, and the place to get the key to the nearby church.

HEALTH AND EMERGENCIES

The symbol displayed outside Greek chemist shops is a red cross on a white ground. The range of non-prescription drugs is wider than in Great Britain. Business hours are equivalent to those of other shops, with Saturday, Sunday and all-night services posted outside. There are hospitals and physicians in all the larger towns.

Hospitals

Chaniá	(0821) 27000
Réthymnon	(0831) 27491
	(0831) 27814
Irákleion	(081) 237502
	(081) 392111
	(081) 229713
Aghios Nikólaos	(0841) 25222

Police

Call toll free on	100

HOLIDAYS AND BUSINESS HOURS

On Greek Orthodox Crete, the movable dates of church holidays (such as the Monday preceding Ash Wednesday, Easter and Whitsun) are determined according to the Julian Calendar and thus seldom coincide with the equivalent holidays of the Roman Catholic and Protestant Churches. The holiest day is Easter, *Pascha*, the culmination of the 40-day fasting period (Lent), and the entire Orthodox year. The Resurrection of Christ is celebrated at midnight by the Orthodox faithful in churches throughout the island.

1 January: New Year's Day

6 January: *Ta Aghia Theofánia*, the blessing of all waters in commemoration of the Baptism of Christ.

Kathará Deftéra: Clean Monday, the Monday preceding Ash Wednesday and the beginning of the fasting period.

25 March: National holiday celebrating the beginning of the struggle against the Turks in 1821.

Megáli Paraskeví: Good Friday, the symbolic Burial of Christ with processions through villages and towns.

Páscha: Comprising Easter Sunday and Monday.

1 May: 'Labour Day' and popular outing day when the people pick flowers and bind them into wreaths to decorate their cars and homes.

Pentecostí: Whit Sunday.

Aghiou Pnévmatos: Whit Monday.

15 August: *Ee Kímissi tis Panagheías*, Assumption of the Virgin Mary, one of the most important holidays.

28 October: National holiday; the Day of *Ohi*, 'no', the Greeks' answer to Mussolini's 1940 ultimatum.

25–26 December: *Christoúyenna*, Christmas.

Shops

All shops are open from 8am–1.30pm, and closed on Monday, Wednesday and Saturday afternoons, as well as all day Sunday. On the other afternoons, the grocers and all the other shops are open 5–8.30pm. Souvenir shops and supermarkets stay open all day and until late in the evening. In the villages, the *kafeneíon* will often double up as the grocery store.

Museums and Excavation Sites

The hours at sites and museums change frequently. Most sites are open in the morning until 2 or 3pm, though closed one weekday. However, except at the major archaelogical sites, it is often possible to wander round outside opening hours, for in many cases there is no perimeter fence. As a rule, monasteries close their doors between noon and 3 or 4pm. Current opening times are included in this guide.

COMMUNICATION AND MEDIA

Media

In all areas catering for tourism, foreign newspapers are available during the tourist season. In major towns, they are on sale all year round at kiosks and bookshops.

Greek radio broadcasts news in English, French and German; television programmes can be received via satellite from other countries.

Telephone (OTE) and Postal Services

In Greece the telephone (OTE) and postal services are handled by separate institutions. Post boxes are yellow, as are the signs outside post offices (*tachythromeía*). In high season, mobile post offices are set up. Post and OTE offices are marked on city maps. Hours of business vary from town to town, but all open 8am–2.30pm. In larger towns offices stay open late in the evening (except on Saturday and Sunday). Phone calls can be made from phone booths and most kiosks: phone cards can be bought at kiosks and OTE offices. Telegrams are sent from OTE offices.

Port Authority

Chaniá (Soúda)	(0821) 89240
Réthymnon	(0831) 28971
Irákleion	(081) 244956
	(081) 244912
Aghios Nikólaos	(0841) 22312

Olympic Airways

Chaniá	(0821) 57701/3
Réthymnon	(0831) 22257
Irákleion	(081) 229191/5
Aghios Nikólaos	(0841) 22033

Road Assistance (toll free)

ELPA	154
Express Service	104
Hellas Service	157

Political billet-doux

Baring all at Préveli

Moní Toploú	91km/57 miles
Palékastro	94km/58 miles
Zákros	110km/68 miles

Hunting

Hunting is very important to Cretan men, perhaps because they were banned from the hunt when the Turks ruled. However, the dramatic reduction of indigenous species, particularly the near extinction of the *krí-krí* wild goat, has led to criticism of hunting.

Mountaineering Clubs

Chaniá	(0821) 44647
Réthymnon	(0831) 57766
Irákleion	(081) 227609

USEFUL INFORMATION

Distances from Chaniá to:

Kastélli/Kissamos	42km/26 miles
Réthymnon	72km/45 miles
Hóra Sfakión	72km/45 miles
Omalós	42km/26 miles
Paleóhora	75km/47 miles

Réthymnon to:

Irákleion	78km/48 miles
Aghía Galíni	62km/39 miles
Amári	39km/24 miles
Moní Préveli	37km/23 miles

Irákleion to:

Aghios Nikólaos	69km/43 miles
Aghios Viánnos	65km/40 miles
Arhánes	13km/8 miles
Festós	62km/39 miles
Kastélli/Pediáda	36km/22 miles
Knossós	5km/3 miles

Aghios Nikólaos to:

Sitía	73km/45 miles
Eloúnda	12km/7 miles
Ierápetra	36km/22 miles
Kritsá	11km/7 miles

Nude Bathing and Rough Camping

Nude bathing (*yimnismós*) and rough camping are prohibited but tolerated at some beaches. Topless sunbathing is common but not encouraged.

Kiosks

Greek life without the *períptero*, or kiosk, would be impossible. They sell essential little things like cigarettes, newspapers, chewing gum, toothpaste, shampoo, aspirin and ballpoint pens until late in the evening. This is where you will also usually find a telephone.

Sport

First and foremost are the watersports (swimming, snorkelling, wind surfing, sailing, etc) and most of the big hotels on the coast hire out equipment. Diving is strictly forbidden because of interest in what sunken archaeological treasures.

Waterparks are popular. Try Aquasplash, close to Hersónissos on road 92 to the Lassíthi Plateau, tel. (0897) 24951, or Water City at Anópolis close to Irákleion, tel. (081) 781316. Both are open closed in winter.

Other popular sports such as tennis are widely available. In the spring and autumn, hiking and climbing in the mountains are particularly attractive.

There are riding stables near Chersónissos and Irákleion. Karterós Horse and Waggon Tours, offering excursions and lessons year round, is based on Karterós Beach, tel. (081) 246035.

Drinking Water

You can drink tap water everywhere except in Irákleion. In the home, drinking water is separate from water for other purposes. It is served with every meal, every sweet dish, each cup of coffee – and is considered a precious treat. Bottled water is available in any small grocers.

The Greek Language

If you take the trouble to learn some Greek prior to embarking on your visit to Crete, you will be rewarded with praise and will make friends more easily. It is a great help to learn the Greek alphabet, even if the majority of street signs are also written in Roman letters. You should have a dictionary and a language guide handy. The *lingua franca* in the tourism sector is English, though German is quickly gaining ground.

Greek is a phonetic language. There are some combinations of vowels and consonants which customarily stand for certain sounds, and some slight pronunciation changes determined by what letter follows but, generally, sounds are pronounced as they are written, without additions or omissions. Thus, learning the phonetic values of the Greek alphabet, and then reading, say, street signs out loud, is a good method of getting the feel of the language.

Most Cretans have some knowledge of English, and most Greeks are delighted to find a visitor making stabs at speaking Greek, even if they are not very successful. The Greeks do not ridicule you for making mistakes: they themselves have a hard time with Greek spelling and the complicated Greek grammar. Whatever you can accomplish, guide book in hand, will be welcomed and rewarded.

In addition to pronouncing each letter, you should remember that stress plays an important role in Modern Greek. When you learn a Greek word, learn where the stress falls at the same time. Each Greek word has a single stress (marked in the following vocabulary list with an accent). Greek is an inflected language as well, and noun and adjective endings change according to gender, number and case. Case endings, the rules governing them and the conjugation of Greek verbs are beyond the scope of a guide and the needs of holidaymakers.

Play on the patio

The Greek Alphabet

CAP.	L.C.	VALUE	NAME
Α	α	a in father	alfa
Β	β	v in visa	vita
Γ	γ	gh before consonants and a, o and oo; y before e, as in year	ghama
Δ	δ	th in then	thelta
Ε	ε	e in let	epsilon
Ζ	ζ	z in zebra	zita
Η	η	e in keep	ita
Θ	θ	th in theory	thita
Ι	ι	e in keep	yota
Κ	κ	k in king	kapa
Λ	l	l in million	lamda
Μ	μ	m in mouse	mi
Ν	ν	n in no	ni
Ξ	ξ	ks in jacks	ksi
Ο	ο	o in oh	omikron
Π	π	p in pebble	pi
Ρ	ρ	r in raisin	ro
Σ	σ	s in sun	sigma
Τ	τ	t in trireme	taf
Ε	ε	e in keep	ipsilon
Φ	φ	f in favor	fi
Χ	χ	h in help	hi
Ψ	ψ	ps in copse	psi
Ω	ω	o in oh	omega

Dipthongs

Type	Value
αι	e in let
αυ	av or af in avert or after
ει	e in keep
ευ	ev or ef
οι	e in keep
ου	oo in poor

Double consonants

μπ	b at beginnings of words; mb in the middle of words
ντ	d at beginnings of words; nd in the middle of words
τζ	dz as in adze
γγ, γκ	gh at the beginnings of words; ng in the middle of words

Vocabulary

Pronounce e as in pet; a as in father; i as in keep; o as in oh.

Numbers

one	é-na (neuter)/ é-nas (masc.)/mí-a(fem.)
two	thí-o
three	trí-a (neuter)/ tris (masc. and fem.)
four	té-se-ra
five	pén-de
six	ék-si
seven	ep-tá
eight	ok-tó
nine	e-né-a
ten	thé-ka
eleven	én-the-ka
twelve	thó-the-ka
thirteen	the-ka-trí-a/the-ka-trís
fourteen	the-ka-té-se-ra
etc. until twenty.	
twenty	í-ko-si
twenty-one	í-ko-si é-na (neuter and masc.) í-ko-si mí-a (fem.)
thirty	tri-án-da
forty	sa-rán-da
fifty	pe-nín-da
sixty	ek-sín-da
seventy	ev-tho-mín-da
eighty	og-thón-da
ninety	e-ne-nín-da
one hundred	e-ka-tó
one hundred and fifty	e-ka-to-pe-nín-da
two hundred	thi-a-kó-si-a (neuter)
three hundred	tri-a-kó-si-a (neuter)
four hundred	te-tra-kó-si-a (neuter)
one thousand	hí-lia (neuter)

Days of the Week

Monday	Thef-té-ra
Tuesday	Trí-ti
Wednesday	Te-tár-ti
Thursday	Pém-pti
Friday	Pa-ras-ke-ví
Saturday	Sá-va-to
Sunday	Ki-ri-a-kí

yesterday kthes
today sí-me-ra
tomorrow á-vri-o

Greetings

Hello yá sas (plural/polite)
yá sou (sing./familiar)
ya (abbreviated)
Good day ká-li mé-ra
Good evening ka-li spe-ra
Good night káli ník-ta
How are you? Ti ká-ne-te? (plural/polite)
Ti ká-nis? (singular/familiar)
fine (in response) ka-lá
pleased to meet you há-ri-ka

Getting Around

yes ne
no ó-hi
okay en dák-si
thank you ef-ha-ris-tó
very much pá-ra po-lí
excuse me sig-nó-mi
it doesn't matter then bi-rá-zi
it's nothing tí-po-ta
certainly/polite yes má-li-sta
Can I..? Bó-ro na..?
When? Pó-te?
Where is..? Pou í-n-e..?
Do you speak English mi-lá-te ta an-gli-ka
What time is it? Ti ó-ra i-ne?
What time will it leave? Ti ó-ra tha fi-gi
I want thé-lo
here/there e-thó/e-kí
small/large mi-kró/me-gá-lo
good/bad ka-ló/ka-kó
warm/cold zes-tó/krí-o
bus le-o-for-í-o
boat ka-rá-vi, va-pó-ri
bike/moped po-thí-la-to/mo-to-po-thí-la-to
ticket i-si-tí-ri-o
road/street thró-mos/o-thós
beach pa-ra-lí-a
sea thá-la-sa
church e-kli-sí-a
ancient ruin ar-hé-a
centre kén-tro
square pla-tí-a

Hotels

hotel kse-no-tho-hí-o
Do you have a room? É-hie-te é-na tho-má-ti-o?
bed kre-vá-ti
shower with hot water douz me zes-tó ne-ró
key kli-thí
entrance í-so-thos
exit ék-so-thos
toilet toua-lé-ta
women's yi-ne-kón
men's án-dron

Shopping

store ma-ga-zí
kiosk pe-ríp-te-ro
open/shut a-nik-tó/klis-tó
post office ta-ki-thro-mí-o
stamp gra-ma-tó-simo
letter grá-ma
envelope fá-ke-lo
telephone ti-lé-fo-no
bank trá-pe-za
marketplace a-go-rá
Have you..? É-hie-te..?
Is there..? É-hi..?
How much does it cost? Pó-so ká-ni?
It's (too) expensive I-ne (po-lí) a-kri-vó
How much? Pó-so?
How many? Pó-sa?

Emergencies

doctor ya-trós
hospital no-so-ko-mí-o
pharmacy far-ma-kí-o
police as-ti-no-mí-a
station stath-mós

'Kalí Stratia' – Farewell

On Crete, when guests depart, they receive a present – a head of cheese, a bag of *paximáthia*, a box full of *kalitsoúnia*, a canister of olive oil, a demijohn of wine, or even *tsigouthiá*. Our gift is a photograph and an anecdote:

A woman, alone in the world (Cháron, the ruler of the Underworld, has taken all her family members), visits the *pappás*, the village priest, and asks, 'Father, father…' 'Go ahead, what do you want?' he replies. 'Can you use *tsigouthiá* as Communion wine?' 'How much have you got?' 'A whole bottle.' 'Oh, then I could use it!' '*Kalí stratia*' is what one wishes someone just before a trip, whether it be short or long: 'good road'. We wish you that, as well, and '*na mas xanártheteh*' – 'visit us again!'

Index

A

B, C

D, E

F

G

H, I, J

K

L

M

N, O

P

R, S

T

V

W, X, Y, Z

NOTES

ACKNOWLEDGMENTS

Photography	María Síri *and*
8/9, 112	Marcus Brooke
55	Regina Hagen
11, 12	Irákleion Museum
2/3	Michelle Macrakis
58	Bill Wassman
108	Hans Wiesenhofer
Handwriting	V Barl
Cartography	Berndtson & Berndtson

NOTES

Notes

NOTES

Notes